Black Tie Optional

A Complete Special Events Resource for Nonprofit Organizations

SECOND EDITION

Black Tie Optional

A Complete Special Events Resource for Nonprofit Organizations

SECOND EDITION

HARRY FREEDMAN
AND KAREN FELDMAN

John Wiley & Sons, Inc.

Library of Congress Cataloging-in-Publication Data:

ISBN 978-0471-70333-4

Printed in the United States of America

10 9 8 7 6 5 4 3 2 1

Contents

About the Authors

Harry Freedman is the President and CEO of Strategic Initiatives based in Philadelphia, Pennsylvania. His company provides fundraising counsel for non profit organizations planning and implementing special events. A fundraising and marketing professional for more than two decades, Freedman is an active member of the Association of Fundraising Professionals, serving on the organization's International Conference and Education Advisory Council. He is also the co-author of two previous books written with Karen Feldman on using business approaches to charitable fundraising. Freedman has been a featured expert in Forbes as well as on NBC's *Dateline* and CNBC.

Karen Feldman is an award-winning journalist whose work has appeared in newspapers and magazines across the United States and Canada. She earned a master's degree at the Columbia University Graduate School of Journalism and worked full-time for daily newspapers for more than 25 years. She lives in Fort Myers, FL.

Acknowledgments

When editor extraordinaire Susan McDermott asked us to revise *Black Tie Optional* for John Wiley & Sons, we took a long time to agree, hoping life would get less complicated and afford us time to write.

We finally realized that wasn't going to happen and decided to give it a try anyway. Through it all, Susan steadfastly supported and encouraged us. Her faith and kindness are largely what inspired us to overcome the obstacles we encountered along the way. We couldn't have done this without her. For her optimism in the face of all evidence to the contrary, she has earned our deepest gratitude.

FROM HARRY FREEDMAN:

This book is dedicated to . . .

Karen Feldman, who is responsible for getting this book into print and for her perseverance and great patience; Susan McDermott, who showed that things often work best when left alone; literary agent Wendy Sherman, who knew exactly what was important and what was not; to my friend and mentor, Richard B. Stolley, for his consistently good advice, long-standing support, and involvement in many of my cause-related projects.

Others to whom I owe thanks include: Hank Lione, Ken Kirby, Shelley Clark, Milt Suchin, Vicki Gilgor, Steve Rovner and Hayes Russock, Ben Protano, Lisa Simon, Beverly Volpe, Joe Farina, Cathy Elkies, and Dr. Joseph Moblio, who through good and bad times have been great sources of inspiration, encouragement, and support.

Much more than an acknowledgment is due philanthropist Dame Celia Lipton Farris, who has given me so many opportunities to work with her and many other celebrities.

I feel lucky and blessed to have worked with Bob and Dolores Hope, Phyllis Diller, Elizabeth Taylor, Tony Bennett, Donald Trump, Dick Clark, Michael J. Fox, Patti Labelle, Kenneth Cole, Joan Rivers, Gloria and Emilio Estefan, Peter Max, Peter Allen, Roberta Flack, and President Bill Clinton, among others. Their participation made it possible to raise millions of dollars for countless worthy causes.

Special thanks are due to several "stars," including my sister, Susan, my nephew, Warren Petrofsky, and his wife, Tracy, who not only shine brightly in my eyes, but know the many times their caring truly made a difference.

To my partner, Paul Siegel, who has been by my side, no matter what, assuring me that the day does not need to be perfect, and that over time love helps you find your way.

Thanks also to Ted Greenberg, Jerry Franks, and Ceilann Boston, for their steadfast loyalty and sustaining friendship.

In the past five years, my family life has greatly changed. This is the spot at which authors usually thank their families. I am thankful for my friends and others who now make up my extended family. They do not replace my biological family, my loving parents and my son, who in the past read their names in this section with proud smiles on their faces, followed by congratulatory hugs. Yet, I see their faces and I feel their hugs and that is truly a special event for me.

FROM KAREN FELDMAN:

I've long suspected that there's a reason book is a four-letter word. Anyone who has ever attempted to produce one knows the travails such a project entails. However, I also believe the process resembles that of childbirth: There may be a great deal of pain, but it's soon forgotten once the labor is over. Many people have generously given of themselves to make this book possible. I owe thanks to:

- The consummate pros who forged a path for us to follow: Editor Susan McDermott and agent Wendy Sherman.

- The experts who shared their knowledge: Barton G. Weiss, Linda Abbey, Shelley Clark, David King, Hank Goldstein, Terry Axelrod, Kenny Rahtz, and Peter Hoogerhuis.
- Harry Freedman, whose diverse and colorful fundraising career forms the basis of this book.
- The people I'm blessed to be able to call friends: Ad Hudler, Dayna Harpster, Donna Forster, and Susan Freedman, all of whom played large parts in making this book a reality.
- My parents, Jerry and Adele Feldman, for their unflagging love and moral support.
- The creatures, furry and otherwise, who share my life and make me laugh no matter how foul my mood: Harry, Gus, Blaze, Nicky, Moorestown, Lily, Nardo, Lolita, Deuce, Marble, Maddie, Goldie, Hattie, Maui, Archie, and Lefty.

Words seem inadequate to express the love and gratitude due my long-suffering and supportive partner, Jim. That he was still willing to marry me after going through the book-writing process is a miracle at which I will always marvel.

Introduction

Charitable fundraising in the 21st century has changed radically from 1990, the year the first edition of this book was published. Back then, there were about 480,000 charities bringing in a total of $114.7 billion a year.

In 2005, Americans donated a record $260.28 billion to some 1 million charitable organizations, according to the Giving USA Foundation. That money came from a variety of sources, including foundations, corporations, and bequests, but the largest slice of the pie—$199 billion—came from individuals who gave to all manner of nonprofit organizations, such as schools, religious institutions, museums, health charities, human service agencies, environmental and animal welfare groups, disaster relief, and international aid. The accompanying chart (Exhibit I.1) shows what portion of donations goes to each sector.

Even though giving is at an all-time high, nonprofit organizations face ever more challenges in raising the money they need to carry out their missions. Americans undergo a constant bombardment by charities attempting to raise money: by mail, e-mail, phone, through the media, and in person. Those seeking to do good appeal to the public in hopes of doing well at securing funds for their causes.

Certified fundraising executive David King, managing partner and president of Alexander Haas Martin & Partners in Atlanta, says that while giving has increased every year since 1930, how groups raise money and where it goes has changed.

There was a time when volunteers—individuals who cared about a cause but did not necessarily have specific expertise in raising money—spearheaded fundraising campaigns. Increasingly, today's fundraisers are paid professionals known as development directors.

EXHIBIT 1.1   GIVING USA FOUNDATION PIE CHART OF WHERE DONATED MONEY GOES

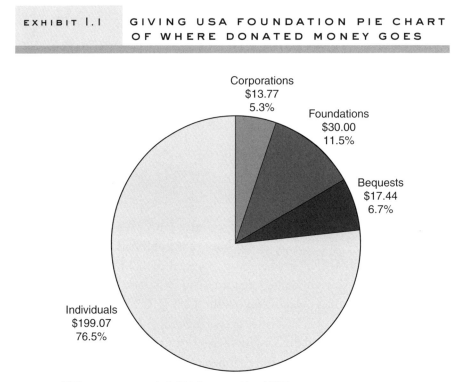

All figures are rounded. Total may not be 100%

"They are starting in at an earlier age and staying in it their entire career. It's really taken off as a profession," King says.

That's changed the ways in which people decide who gets their charitable dollars.

"The percentage to religious groups gets smaller," he says. "It used to be 50 percent went to religious groups but, by 2004, it was about 30 percent."

King believes that "some of that is related to the fact that churches have not yet gone the paid-professional route when it comes to fundraising. They don't do the professional, systematic, process-driven work that other types of groups are doing.

"There's a lot more competition. The field is getting much more professional . . . People are being approached for a lot of different things. How they're approached and how they are treated after the gift is playing a bigger and bigger role in what they give the next time around," King says.

It's increasingly common for more than one organization to take aim at a particular cause. When that happens, it can pose a hardship for all of the groups struggling to raise money and, all too often, they wind up competing for the same pool of donors.

ACCOUNTABILITY

Most donors want to know that their gifts will be spent wisely. Rather than relying on the recipient's word that the charity will make the most of donations, people want proof that their money is being used judiciously. Providing that proof, building public confidence in the charity, is essential.

Only 15 percent of Americans had a great deal of trust in charities, according to a 2005 study conducted by New York University's Robert F. Wagner School of Public Service. Nearly half of those surveyed had a fair amount of confidence in charities, 24 percent expressed little confidence, and 7 percent had none at all.

That means that even nonprofit groups working for worthy causes have to sell themselves to their potential donors in the same way that retail businesses do, including making sure that donors believe they are getting good value for their investment. It's all about credibility.

Independent Sector (www.independentsector.org), a coalition of charities and foundations based in Washington, D.C., has developed a "Checklist for Accountability" that advises nonprofits to:

- Develop a culture of accountability and transparency.
- Adopt a statement of values and a code of ethics.
- Adopt a specific conflict-of-interest policy.
- Conduct independent financial reviews, especially audits, and make findings available to the public.
- Create a whistleblower-protection policy to prevent retribution against those who report possible misconduct or malfeasance.
- Ensure the board of directors understands and is capable of fulfilling its financial responsibilities.

These principles are somewhat general, but when followed along with standards recommended by the Better Business Bureau's Wise Giving

Alliance (www.give.org), charities can be fairly confident that they meet the industry's generally accepted standards.

GuideStar (www.guidestar.org) is a nonprofit dedicated to helping improve other nonprofit groups' public image. It maintains a large database containing information on more than 1 million organizations, all of which are encouraged to provide complete details on their finances and practices. Groups striving to build credibility should aim to be totally transparent, detailing the organization's financial state, how money is spent, and where it goes. This information should be on the charity's own Web site as well as sites such as GuideStar so potential donors with the inclination can educate themselves before deciding whether to write that check. Keep in mind the expectations of potential donors when crafting the charity's online message (see Exhibit I.2).

Only after establishing itself as a reputable, responsible organization should any nonprofit take on the job of producing a special event and, even then, it's not the answer for every group. Those that do choose to raise money through special events need to consider more than simply what sort to hold: They need to give careful thought to why they are doing it and what they hope to accomplish.

"I think people are really trying to move away from special events as fundraisers and starting to view them as friend raisers," says King. "A lot of organizations we work with are looking at special events very critically now, deciding which to keep and which to let go. They need to focus on quality rather than quantity. I see a lot of organizations really turning toward major gift fund raising.

"People are a little bit exhausted from events. In Atlanta, you can go to a gala every single Saturday. Organizations really need to look at what kind of event is appropriate for their mission."

Barton Weiss, the head of Barton G., a Miami-based production, catering, and restaurant empire, says he believes galas still have value.

"Why not just donate and be done?" he says. "Because people want a return on their dollar, they want some fulfillment."

Peter Hoogerhuis is the vice president of marketing for Auctionpay, a company that helps nonprofits process payments for auctions and other special events and offers a suite of fundraising software.

He says special events also "provide a great fundraising source that's not only good money but it's unrestricted funds. A lot of nonprofits will tell

EXHIBIT 1.2 DONORS' TOP 10 EXPECTATIONS—
CHRONICLE OF PHILANTHROPY

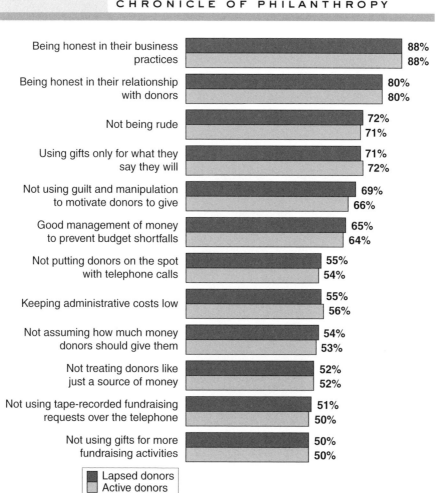

you that foundation money and grant money is very specifically focused on certain programs."

In their zeal to fund the group's project, entities awarding these restricted funds may leave a charity without enough for administrative costs. Money raised through special events can fill that void.

But in today's super-competitive fundraising climate, it's not enough to give potential donors a good time. Focus on the mission, not the party, says Terry Axelrod, CEO and founder of Raising More Money, an organization devoted to helping nonprofits achieve sustainable funding.

Groups intent on staging special events should "be sure whatever event you have includes your mission," she advises. "Do a 10-minute segment where you educate people about your work. (People) shouldn't just dance, drink or play golf. A nonprofit should not be in the business of entertaining. People should go away and remember something. That's the test we use. They should be able to remember the name of the organization and be able to tell a friend something about it the next day."

She recommends that an organization produce a short informational video or DVD to show at events or bring in people who have benefited from the group's work to provide short, personal testimonials that will make an impression upon those in attendance.

If the presentation succeeds, those who attended "should be inspired and should tell other people about you," Axelrod says. "Otherwise, why do an event?"

Organizations seeking to stay current should have their own Web sites that they update frequently. The site should clearly explain the group's mission and needs, provide testimonials and photos of recipients of that aid, a copy of the annual budget, and a button people can click on to donate online.

Just like good investors, nonprofits must diversify when it comes to fundraising strategies. King says he works with some groups that rely heavily on a single, highly lucrative event each year to fund the lion's share of their budgets. But some unforeseen, uncontrollable factor can change everything.

He cites an AIDS service organization that traditionally relied on a single outdoor event each year to bring in 50 percent of its income. The event usually attracted tens of thousands of participants and raised lots of money. But what happens the year it rains on that date? It's not simply the event that's a washout—it could potentially bring down the organization.

Groups such as this one need diverse funding sources, including an annual fund, a major gifts program, and a big annual fundraiser to protect itself from financial ruin.

Charities must also change with the times, says Hank Goldstein, president and chief executive officer of the Oram Group, a consulting firm for philanthropic organizations.

"There's a lot of fickleness in philanthropy, both in the short term and the long term," he says. "HIV-AIDS was big 10 to 15 years ago, but those groups are now having a terrible time trying to raise money. The emphasis has shifted."

In 2006, battling breast cancer was a far more popular cause.

Advances in technology have allowed for a vast expansion of global philanthropy. Groups from India, Africa, China, and Europe are adopting American fundraising techniques and going after some of the same dollars. And, although Americans donated roughly $650 million to aid victims of the Asian tsunami in 2004 and early 2005, Goldstein points out that that represents an infinitesimal portion of Americans' charitable donations. He attributes that outpouring, in part, to the fact that it occurred just after Christmas. In general, Americans give only a small amount to foreign causes.

But as the U.S. population changes, patterns of giving change, too. Huge numbers of people from India and Central and South America are moving to the United States. Many of these new immigrants are likely to send money back to their native countries rather than donating to American organizations that solicit them in the traditional ways.

The bottom line: Leaders of charitable organizations must develop multi-dimensional, long-term strategies for raising money. These may include joining forces with other groups that have similar or compatible missions. For many that will still include special events, but those events must be more judiciously selected and tailored to the specific audience, rather than relying on the fact that people have turned up in previous years.

They must work smarter, too, using new tools made possible by the Internet and high-powered computer technology, while being careful not to rely on them too heavily.

This book aims to help today's fundraisers—both professionals and volunteers—pick the events that best suit them and make the most money from those they choose to produce. Great special events involve little magic: They are business undertakings, brought about through organization, sufficient numbers of workers (paid and otherwise), a realistic budget, and large quantities of patience and hard work. This book's goal is to demystify the process and make it as easy as possible to succeed in the business of special events.

CHAPTER 1

Choosing the Right Event

Considering how much manpower and money it takes to produce a special event, there are only three good reasons to have one:

1. To raise money
2. To raise the group's profile
3. To attract new members/donors

In deciding what type of event to hold, first pinpoint the group's target market and then compile a list of events likely to appeal to that demographic.

Ask people who attend a lot of events which they found most memorable. Look at other events held locally and further afield to figure out which are the most financially successful and whether they might be a good fit.

Look for fundraisers that have succeeded elsewhere by searching the Web for major charity events in comparable communities. Check the society or lifestyles sections of newspapers and magazines in those areas, as well as those in major metropolitan areas, such as New York City, Chicago, Denver, and Los Angeles. Look in their archives for events held at the same time the previous year.

Groups just entering the fundraising arena should limit their choices to events that require a modest amount of manpower and up-front money.

Choosing an event that has some novelty to it yet appeals to a broad range of ages and interests can take lots of brainstorming, but that's what most groups should aim for.

That's why auctions have become such popular events in recent years. An auction of sought-after goods—celebrity items, special dinners at private homes, travel packages, jewelry—combined with an hors d'oeuvres or dessert buffet, has the potential to raise as much or more money than the standard dinner-dance. An auction with hors d'oeuvres costs substantially less than a sit-down meal with dancing. The pace of an auction is livelier so guests are apt to enjoy it more. That's likely to translate into more generous bids and greater profits. (For more details, see Chapter 8, Auctions and Other Profit Boosters.)

Because of the nature of auctions—the ability to make them longer or shorter based on the number of items available and to offer a range of items that appeals to many tastes—they fit easily into many other events. With appealing prizes and a motivated work force, an auction can generate a substantial amount of money. However, live auctions require lots of workers and lots of items and so aren't the best choices for novice groups.

For a first-time event, choose one that area residents would attend even if it weren't for charity. That makes promotion easier. So does coming up with something different from the pack, possibly a performance by a high-profile, in-demand speaker.

Bringing in a well-known personality to speak can be relatively easy to do and can also provide a welcome change of pace from dances and galas. It's an effective way to attract new donors and offers loads of opportunities for corporate sponsorship. Next to auctions, it ranks among the most profitable events there are. A noteworthy speaker can quickly and easily sell out the house.

If a group member is acquainted with someone who would draw a crowd, have that member make the request personally. For everyone else there are speakers' bureaus, such as the Greater Talent Network (www.greatertalent.com) and the Harry Walker Agency (www.harrywalker.com), both in New York City, and Celebrity Talent International (www.celebritytalent.net) in California. These networks represent hundreds of authors, politicians, athletes, artists, actors, and well-known print and TV journalists, as well as others who speak compellingly about wellness, culture, media, technology, and a host of other current topics. Such companies can help match a group with a speaker uniquely suited to its particular mission and budget.

"If it's cancer related, Katie Couric is a good choice because she's so dedicated to the cause," says Kenny Rahtz, Greater Talent Network's senior vice president. "Just about every celebrity has two or three organizations to which they dedicate a good amount of time and can be counted upon for making speeches and attending major fundraising events."

But such luminaries do not come cheap. Couric charges upwards of $100,000 to appear. She donates her fees to cancer research. Speaker fees start at about $5,000 and go up, Rahtz says. The bigger the name, generally the higher the fee.

> **TIP** *Sometimes nonprofit organizations can get a lower price. It doesn't hurt to ask.*

Celebrity Talent International differs from other groups in that it represents the charities, rather than the celebrities, and so attempts to get nonprofits the best rates available. It has connections to many speakers, singers, and other performers that its staff helps match to a charity's needs. It also offers advice on acquiring sponsors to offset costs, will supply prior to signing a contract a summary of average costs of the technical equipment the performer will need, and can also provide full production and technical services when needed.

The advantage to spending money on a speaker rather than another dinner-dance is that each event can be different. The group can book one speaker for an evening, or a few for a full-day event with multiple breakout sessions, or a series of speakers throughout the year.

Speakers' bureaus help schedule events and some also coordinate advance news coverage. Members of the news media can call the network and someone on staff will arrange advance phone interviews with the speaker, significantly increasing publicity without additional cost or effort on the part of the charity's staff and volunteers. A speakers' bureau might also handle travel arrangements for the speaker.

> **TIP** *Don't be afraid to ask questions, including what the total cost will be.*

Festivals centered on popular foods generally draw good-sized crowds. Foods such as chocolate, chili, or seafood are always winners. So are gatherings of well-known area chefs or popular area restaurants offering their specialties. The charity raises money from admission fees, tickets for food and drinks, a raffle, a silent auction, a celebrity dunk tank, and a program and advertising booklet. These events can raise a sweet $100,000 or more —assuming there's a good turnout and organizers are vigilant about keeping expenses low.

Other popular events include home tours, designer homes, golf tournaments, and other sporting events.

While the event needs broad appeal, it should also include something that will attract people with its novelty, perhaps something that's been done elsewhere but not locally or something that brings together a number of desirable elements not normally found together. And if it's something for which demand exceeds supply, so much the better.

That's what the Central Park Conservancy did when it hosted its Blue Moon Gala. The event was held at Tavern on the Green, the renowned Central Park restaurant transformed by flamboyant restaurateur Warner LeRoy, who spent $10 million renovating it.

LeRoy underwrote most of the expenses for the gala that was to help the conservancy restore Central Park. He had thousands of sapphire lights hung throughout the restaurant. He brought in *60 Minutes* correspondents Morley Safer, Steve Kroft, Ed Bradley, and Andy Rooney, as well as Charlie Rose and the late Peter Jennings. The conservancy held an all-blue fashion show, hired the Mambo Kings to perform, and arranged for magicians and a fire-breather to roam the crowd.

The group limited the number of tickets available, making them all the more exclusive and appealing. The result: 750 socialites attended, and the event raised $1 million for the conservancy, says Shelley Clark, vice president of Lou Hammond and Associates, who helped create and promote the gala.

Another success story is that of a long-running event at Penn State University known as THON. It began as a fairly simple weekend-long dance-a-thon to benefit The Four Diamonds Fund, which helps provide care for children with cancer, support for their families, and research at Penn State Children's Hospital at Hershey Medical Center in Hershey, PA.

Over the years, it has become one of the largest student-run philanthropic groups in the country, raising close to $42 million over 30 years. THON 2006 brought in a record $4.21 million, the result of a year-long fundraising effort that involved some 10,000 students and supporters.

Long before the main event in February, organizers stage several other events to raise money. There's a phone-a-THON to alumni, a THON 5K, a family carnival, a kickoff dinner, and fundraising workshops. They sell THON family and friends' cookbooks, stickers, and blue plastic THON wristbands that read "For the kids."

The fundraising year culminates with hundreds of students participating in the no-sitting, no-sleeping, 48-hour dance-a-thon, while thousands of spectators cheer them on. (See www.thon.org for details.)

While THON has taken on a life of its own that helps keep momentum flowing from year to year, most events need a serious push and careful oversight by organizers. The best way to ensure a successful charity event is to treat it like any other business undertaking: Assess the market, develop a detailed plan and budget, and continuously build the donor (customer) base. Read on for ways to do this.

MARKETING

What do mood rings, pet rocks, and Cabbage Patch dolls have in common? Each enjoyed monumental, if fleeting, popularity. The makers of these products struck upon something novel that appealed to consumers, albeit briefly. That's the challenge today's charities face in raising money: figuring out what the public wants and then delivering it.

That's what market research is all about and it's every bit as important for charities as it is in the private sector. The organization has to make a profit or, like any other business, it will fail.

Long before a charity stages an event, the leaders must assess the community, its tastes, and spending habits. Knowing the market will make all of the group's events more successful.

First, look closely at the organization:

- How many reliable volunteers are there?
- How much experience does the group have at fundraising?
- What events has the group successfully produced before?

- Who attended those events?
- Which is more important to the group right now: raising money or building awareness of the cause?
- How much corporate sponsorship is available?
- What about individual major donors?
- How successful has the group been in conveying its cause and mission and has the community signed on?
- What has the group invested (spent on specific events) versus what it raised?

Besides holding fundraising events, keeping the organization in the public eye is vitally important. Set up a schedule of written news releases as well as TV and radio public service announcements. Look for local cable shows with logical tie-ins and use a Web site, blogs, and e-mail to get the word out about the group's cause, goals, and successes.

Animal Haven Shelter (www.animalhavenshelter.org) in Flushing, N.Y, raised $60,000 in Katrina relief donations, in large part because of blog entries by the organization's executive director, Marcello Forte, who participated in the rescue efforts and wrote about it from the field. The group also sent out a series of e-mails in the weeks after the disaster that included special reports and pictures from the field. And it maintains a Web page called Success Stories that displays photos and stories of rescued Katrina animals with their adoptive families. To educate donors as to how their money is spent, the cover story of *The Animal Haven Journal* Winter 2006 edition was entitled: "Volunteers S-T-R-E-T-C-H Donor Dollars." Also on the Web site is a place to click to donate money. This is an organization that makes it easy for supporters to give.

Other ways to keep the group's name in front of potential supporters include:

- Hold regular information meetings and awareness-building events for the public and news media highlighting the charity's mission.
- Sponsor a sports team or youth group.
- Encourage supporters to host small gatherings at their homes to introduce friends and colleagues to the cause. If members have already

educated others about the cause, earning their interest and loyalty, they can concentrate on raising money when event time comes.

When setting out to raise money, a charity sells its image right along with tickets.

So how does a group come up with that one event that will make a splash? There are lots of resources available. Search the Internet for successful events. Use a search engine to research terms such as "fundraising events" or "charitable events." Read the society pages of local newspapers and magazines. Flip through magazines such as *People*, *Entertainment Weekly*, *Us*, and *In Style*. Check out what's covered on television programs such as *Entertainment Tonight*. All should provide fodder for interesting, creative events.

Pay attention to which celebrities and corporations actively support which efforts. Make a list and update it regularly. (More on celebrities in Chapter 9, Reaching for the Stars.)

SAMPLE EVENTS

Following are some fundraising ideas (listed alphabetically). Each idea includes some pros and cons, an estimate of staff and planning time required, and costs associated with that particular event.

To estimate actual costs, put together a preliminary budget using the worksheet in Chapter 2, Money Matters. Make sure to add any special costs associated with the event under consideration. Completing the budget accurately is essential for determining whether the event is within the organization's means. There are lots of variables: whether it's a first-time event or a repeat of an event that's built a following; how much underwriting or sponsorship the group can obtain; and whether insurance, such as liability, fire, and weather, might be needed.

Drawing up a preliminary budget will help determine the amount of staff and volunteer time required. Count the number of committees and the tasks each one must complete. Figure out how many people each committee will need to get the work done, then add 10 percent, so work loads won't be overwhelming and there will be enough manpower even when some volunteers drop out and others prove less productive than expected.

> **TIP**   *Plan on one worker for every 50 participants for an event listed as "moderate" in people needs. Add more for events requiring "high" amounts of manpower, less for those listed as "minimal."*

Don't dismiss smaller events out of hand as not worth the effort. It might be more lucrative and less taxing for the group to stage several, less-complicated events over the year, bringing in $10,000 each time, rather than spending six months planning a huge, expensive event that might bring in only marginally more than that. Given the uncertainty of the nation's economy in recent years, many people are reluctant to attend high-end balls and concerts, and many major companies, which have traditionally provided the bulk of underwriting and sponsorship money, may be downsizing personnel and philanthropic efforts.

Considering how ubiquitous the Internet has become, don't forget to examine the group's potential for raising money online, both through its Web site and those of others, such as eBay (more on that in Chapter 8, Auctions and Other Profit Boosters).

Here's a sampling of events that are possible, but there are far too many to include them all. Roam the Internet for more examples of what others have done.

Antique Show

Sign up as many area antique dealers as possible. Charge each for a booth or space. Charge an admission fee to the public. On opening night, set a higher ticket price for those who want the first shot at merchandise. Sell food and beverages. Hold a raffle and create a program book.

> **Planning time:** Three months for a small show, as much as 12 months for a large one
>
> **People needs:** Moderate. One person to round up vendors and dealers, another to manage the site and publicity, one to acquire raffle items, one or more to sell ads in the program book. Others to help staff the event, set up and clean up afterward.
>
> **Costs:** Budget money for security because of the value of the items involved.

Arts and Crafts Show

These range from small, simple affairs featuring homemade crafts, to grand showcases, such as Miami Beach's Art Deco Weekend, which attracts thousands of people every January. A small show can come together in a couple of months, while large-scale events such as Art Deco Weekend are year-round projects. Go to other craft fairs and give out registration forms for the group's forthcoming show, collect cards from vendors, and search on the Internet for craftsmen and artists who travel to shows outside of their area. Use these to create a master list.

Planning time: Three to four months

People needs: Minimal to high. Two or three people can handle a small show, with one signing up artists and one handling staging. A larger show might require 20 to 40 workers divided into committees to handle artists, publicity, staging/set-up, entertainment, food vendors, raffles, program book, and cleanup.

Costs: Long before the event date nears, the group will need money and publicity to attract and sign a sufficient number of artists.

A-Thons

There's hardly an activity that hasn't been made into an "a-thon." Aerobics, bowling, car racing, bicycling, cooking, running, rocking, haircutting, dancing, jumping rope, kissing, singing, swimming, skating, skateboarding, walking, wheelchairing, and wheelbarrowing have all been used to good effect. Participants solicit pledges from people prior to the event. Generally the amount pledged depends on how long the person performs the designated activity or it is calculated by score (ten cents per bowling pin struck down or swim lap completed). Obviously, the more participants who collect pledges, the larger the profit will likely be. To stimulate friendly competition, encourage people to enter as teams (friends, co-workers, members of other groups), each with a captain, with prizes for both individuals and teams that raise the most. There are a couple of drawbacks to consider: Weather can wash away the competition for some of the activities. Another is that this is an often-used activity and boredom may set in among those who would ordinarily take part. Check around to see if other, more established, local groups are sponsoring these. If so, consider changing events or partnering with a group that already stages one. This type of event relies heavily on publicity and word of mouth and tends to grow each year. One way to boost media coverage is to get one or more media personalities to participate.

And one more caveat: Some cities are not as welcoming to walk-a-thons and the like as they once were. Having hundreds—or thousands—of people coursing through the streets creates traffic interruptions, puts walkers at risk, and creates logistical nightmares for law enforcement. Groups wishing to stage a walk-a-thon should first look for a large park or other off-the-street venue in which to hold it. That's likely to make officials more welcoming—and more likely to grant the group's request to hold one. However, some cities are even limiting these because the large events keep others from enjoying the parks. Check to make sure it's possible to hold one in a specific spot before scheduling the event.

Planning time: Three to six months

People needs: Moderate. This requires volunteers to line up participants, distribute pledge forms, make follow-up calls, conduct signup, and track pledge sheets and donations.

Costs: Allow ample money for advance costs, such as insurance, permits, site expenses, T-shirts, giveaways, sign-up and pledge sheets, advertising and publicity, and awards. Save some money for an accountant if there isn't one in the group and always leave several thousand dollars for next year's start-up expenses.

Auctions

These can center on celebrity items, tickets to concerts or sporting events, cars, people, travel, food, restaurant meals, art, jewelry—whatever a committee can convince people to donate to a worthy cause. Live auctions are among the most labor-intensive fundraisers, especially if there are a lot of items for live auction as well as a silent auction. Always make sure that the auction items match the spending power of those attending. Far less costly and less laborious is an online auction, via a program such as eBay's Giving Works, which allows charities to auction items and lets individuals who are selling items designate that a particular charity receive a set portion of the sale price. (See Chapter 8, Auctions and Other Profit Boosters, for details.)

Planning time: Six months or more for the live variety; about a month or two for online (including collecting items to sell)

People needs: High for live events. Auctions require many people to procure the items, set up and work the room, and make sure people with money to spend attend the event. Online auctions require several people collecting items, some to e-mail donors alerting them to the auction, someone to handle the online listings, and a few to handle billing and shipping.

Costs: Because items must be collected in advance of the event, include money in the budget for storage rental, security, and liability insurance.

Balloon Races

This is an event that is totally dependent on Mother Nature's mood. It requires a big open field, several hot-air balloonists and their balloons, perfect weather with no wind, and a good crowd. These are sometimes held on the site of a shopping mall before construction begins. Other possibilities include farm fields, large parks, and the lawns of large estates. Sell sponsorships on balloons, charge admission to watch, sell food, hold a raffle, sell photos of people standing in the balloon baskets. A caveat: This can be a risky event, given the vicissitudes of the weather.

Planning time: Three months

People needs: Minimal by hiring a professional group of balloonists or a balloon club to handle things; don't even think about doing this one without the experts.

Costs: Insurance and site rental. Set up food booths at the beginning and ending sites (although landing sites are notoriously difficult to predict). A major corporate sponsor is essential for this event's success. Approach new stores, hotels and restaurants, radio or television stations and ask that they pledge money to pay for the event, with proceeds going to the charity.

Beach Party

This one's a no-brainer for coastal communities. It's an ideal event for attracting families and younger people who may then choose to get involved in the cause as a result. If there isn't a handy beach nearby, truck in a load of sand and create one, complete with potted faux palm trees. When using real beaches, make sure to acquire all the necessary permits from whichever agency oversees that particular stretch of sand. Line up popular bands to perform. Charge admission. Organize a volleyball tournament with entry fees and cash prizes. Depending on the crowd, hold an ugly bartender contest, and perhaps a "babes" and "hunks" competition, in which people pay $5 to vote. Bring in vendors to sell refreshments. The beer concession can be a major moneymaker so a beer sponsor can make a big difference in how much the charity makes, especially if the sponsoring beverage company donates all or part of the beer proceeds in exchange for being named a sponsor in advertisements and banners. Get a radio station to broadcast live to encourage greater turnout. Some stations will serve as sponsors and provide free on-air publicity for the event.

Planning time: Four or five months

People needs: High. People are needed to set everything up and procure sponsors, vendors, and music. On the day of the event, there must be workers to handle security and crowd control, staff booths, sell food and T-shirts, collect tickets, direct parking, and clean up.

Costs: Weather is the biggest risk so buy inclement weather insurance along with a liability policy.

Bingo

In places in which bingo is legal, there are usually bingo halls—places that do nothing but hold bingo games. In most states, a portion of every session must benefit a charity. Check those in the area to see if there's a session open that the group could claim.

Planning time: Four months

People needs: Minimal if using an established bingo hall. Usually a volunteer from the charity must be present during the session. People needs are higher if there are no bingo halls and the group has to produce its own game and attract the players.

Costs: Allow a generous publicity fund. Bingo does best with lots of advance notice.

Book or CD Signings

Many major book and music stores sponsor signings by artists and authors. These generally aren't great moneymakers, but can be good vehicles for promotion. Tie in a raffle, perhaps awarding a meal with the featured writer or artist. Other possibilities include signed copies of the person's book, CD, limited edition poster, or original work of art.

Planning time: One to three months

People needs: Minimal. Someone needs to set the time and location, book the author or artist, handle publicity, and help out at the event. If there's going to be a raffle, people are needed to gather the items.

Costs: Check to see if the store or person appearing requires that the group purchase a minimum amount of merchandise. If so, include that in the budget.

Business Opening/Store and Mall Events

A store, restaurant, nightclub, supermarket, office building, or mall can be a great place to stage an event. In some cases, the company's employees or advertising firm will handle the planning and publicity, leaving the charity to concentrate on delivering guests with significant disposable income. In return, many businesses will pay for printing, ads, giveaways and sometimes even the food. The more successful the charitable organization is in bringing in well-heeled potential customers, the more likely it will be asked to participate in future openings. If the charity can't attract 600 affluent people for a grand opening, don't try this. This is an easy event to produce so there's usually stiff competition. The group needs a top-notch, professional proposal to present to the business and the ability to deliver the turnout and sales it promises in order to successfully compete against other charities. If the group can't muster the requisite number of customers, consider partnering with one or more other nonprofit groups. Whatever profit there is gets divided evenly among the groups but so, too, do expenses.

If the charity can bring in a celebrity (local or otherwise), so much the better. (See Chapter 9, Reaching for the Stars.) When working with a mall, make sure there's one person in charge who speaks for all the stores.

Shopping Day: A variation on this is a shopping day, in which supporters of a particular charity are invited to shop (or dine) on a specific day, with a percentage of proceeds to benefit the charity (or charities). The business promotes the event in its ads and may offer discounts on some or all of its merchandise to shoppers who have special passes. The charities sell one-day shopping passes (priced at $5 to $10) to supporters for that day, with a different color pass for each group, allowing the stores to properly credit sales. Supporters can take advantage of discounts and help their favorite charities by shopping during the event.

Planning time: Three months

People needs: Minimal for the charity if the business' employees get involved. Moderate if group members must to do the advance work themselves.

Costs: Minimal. The new business should pick up most of the costs.

Car/Bike Shows

Antique, vintage, specific makes, RVs, sports cars, or motorcycles all have passionate devotees. Get the local club of car or motorcycle enthusiasts involved or find a promoter who will organize the show while group members handle publicity and sell tickets. Don't forget to include the always popular—and lucrative—raffle and program book. If there's someone in the group who's a particularly good negotiator or has ties to a local auto or motorcycle dealer, have that person approach the company management and ask them to donate a vehicle to be raffled off. In exchange, the company gets prominent mention in all promotional material and at the event itself. Sell raffle tickets for $100 each, limiting the number sold (to 500 or so). It's a great way to boost the event's bottom line.

Planning time: Three to six months

People needs: Minimal. The group will need to be on hand to guide crowds and parking, as well as supervise and collect money at the event.

Costs: Take out inclement weather insurance and coverage for the cars.

Casino Nights

Most organizations hire a company that does this professionally. That's because it's apt to cost more for the group to rent the equipment and hire the dealers on its own than to engage a firm that does this on a regular basis. It's a somewhat pricey but easy event to hold because the organization is essentially buying it whole. The group will have to arrange for the prizes, printing, publicity, and sale of tickets. If there are casino boats in the area, check on chartering one for an afternoon or evening, or charging a higher price than usual for a designated sailing with the extra money going to the charity. Then the group just has to sell tickets.

Planning time: Four to six months

People needs: High for self-produced casino nights on land; moderate if using a pro; minimal for a gambling cruise.

Costs: Don't skimp on security.

Celebrity Appearances

This is for seasoned fundraisers only. Novices should not attempt this on their own. Finding a celebrity (such as a singer, musician, or dancer) who will appear at a price the group can afford is the key to success here. Consult a lawyer (one who donates time to the group is ideal, but hire one otherwise) to make sure the contract is suitable. Scour the fine print for hidden expenses and clauses that may allow the celebrity to cancel at the last minute, if offered a film role, TV appearance, etc. Deploy as many volunteers as possible to sell tickets.

Groups new to large-scale fundraising might want to purchase a block of tickets to an appearance someone else is producing, then sell them at a higher price with the difference going to the charity. Check with large local venues for a group sales department. Purchasing tickets through that department means the group will get a discount, the amount of which varies according to the group size and date of performance. If possible, boost fundraising by holding a meet-the-celebrity reception following the show, charging an additional fee.

Planning time: At least six months

People needs: Moderate. Volunteers or staff must book the location and the celebrity, handle contracts, and tend to the celebrity's needs. Others are needed to sell tickets and publicize the event.

Costs: Make sure there's money available for advance publicity and deposits.

Chili Cookoff

Connect with a regional or national chili competition, then line up contestants, each of whom pays an entrance fee, and find a spot to hold it. If the public is going to purchase samples of the food, the site will have to meet health department guidelines, which isn't easy to do outside the confines of a commercial kitchen. It's best to hire a restaurant known for its chili to come in and serve portions customers can buy. (This also works with gumbo, chowder, baked goods, and other popular foods.) Charge admission, hold a raffle. Enlist a radio or television station to serve as a sponsor. Getting a corporate sponsor to cover the cost of entertainment is always a plus. Try connecting with a beer or bottled water company looking to promote new products to serve as yet an additional sponsor.

Planning time: Four to six months

People needs: Moderate to high. This isn't a good event for a two-person office to try to pull off. Cookoffs require committees to sign up competitors, handle publicity, site acquisition, entertainment, security, and parking.

Costs: Equipment and booth rental quickly add up. Event and liability insurance are musts.

Concert (Local Talent)

Count on this sort of show to be more of a profile builder than a money-maker. Hold it in a school auditorium or church sanctuary and publicize it through the school or church newsletter, in addition to the standard spots (newspaper, radio, newsletter, Web sites, e-mail). To boost profits, sell beverages, baked goods and/or candy and hold a raffle before and after the show (and during intermission if there is one).

Planning time: One to three months

People needs: Moderate. There must be people to sell tickets, book the talent and location, and orchestrate the raffle and food sales.

Costs: Moderate. If the venue isn't donated, there's the site rental plus the usual printing of tickets and programs.

Concert (Celebrity)

For groups just starting out, it is far easier and less risky to purchase a block of tickets to an already scheduled performance. Sell them at a higher price, with the difference going to the charity. Only a well-established organization with ample advance money available and a loyal base of supporters should attempt to produce its own concert.

Planning time: Three months to sell tickets to someone else's show; six months or more for the charity to produce its own

People needs: Moderate with a few people needed to sell tickets to an already scheduled show; high for groups going it alone.

Costs: Moderate to high. The group will need to pay for a variety of items, including advertising, site deposits, and such if going it alone. If selling tickets to someone else's concert, the group will have to buy tickets in advance.

Cooking Demonstration

Arrange to have chefs appear at a local department store (in the housewares department) or at a restaurant or cooking school when the establishment normally is closed. People pay to see the demonstration. The charity might pick up extra money if it gets a percentage based on the value of merchandise sold during the show. If the chef has published a cookbook, have the author sign copies there and try to get a percentage of the book sales, too.

Planning time: About three months

People needs: Minimal

Costs: Very little if the store or restaurant will pay for advertising, or will contribute to the cost of producing and sending out invitations.

Costume Party

Allow guests to choose any identity they wish or use a theme (TV characters, colors, a time period) or occasion (Halloween, Mardi Gras, Christmas in July, etc.). Increase profits with a program book, raffle, and auction.

Planning time: Three to six months

People needs: Minimal to moderate depending on how elaborate the party is. The group needs people to address invitations, serve refreshments, find a site, and handle publicity, as well as some to oversee the party itself.

Costs: Moderate. Invitations (generally done in-house on the office computer), tickets, postage, renting a site, refreshments.

County Fair/Carnival/Street Fair

Have a variety of booths featuring arts and crafts, food, and music. Volunteers can construct the booths. To boost attendance, bring in other attractions, such as 4-H displays, appearances by local school choirs, orchestras, and marching bands. Have pig or crab races. This will do more to promote the group's image than increase its operating revenue. Consider tying in with another organization's festival or "a-thon" to cut costs and expose more people to the cause. Some municipalities help sponsor such events by waiving rental fees on a park or recreation center.

Planning time: Two to four months

People needs: High. Lots of volunteers are needed to set up booths, attract vendors, arrange for entertainment, handle tickets, parking, and cleanup.

Costs: Enough upfront money to cover booth rental, site cleanup, security, and insurance.

Cow-Chip Bingo

This simple event requires one well-fed cow delivered to a football field or other large area divided into one-square-yard plats. Sell plats for $30 and include a meal (barbecue, subs, etc.) in the price. Release a well-fed cow onto the field and allow her to wander at will until she drops her, uh, chips. The owner of the splat-upon plat wins. Charge non-plat holders admission, sell refreshments, give away prizes, hold a raffle.

Planning time: Two months

People needs: Moderate. Workers are needed to find the site and arrange for a cow to be delivered (and returned), sell tickets and plats, handle publicity, and run things during the event itself.

Costs: Cow rental, possibly site rental, weather insurance.

Cruise

There are four variations:

1. **A full-length cruise.** Arrange with a cruise line or travel agent to sell tickets for a particular cruise with a percentage of the price going to the charity. To attract wealthy older people, pick a longer cruise that travels to exotic, out-of-the-ordinary ports. For a young crowd, opt for a shorter, less costly voyage.

   Planning time: Four to six months

   People needs: Minimal. The group supplies people to publicize the trip and sell tickets. The cruise line takes care of virtually everything else.

   Costs: Private parties and shore excursions will add to expenses. Include them in the ticket price.

2. **A cruise with special benefits for the group.** Some cruise lines offer charities special packages. The cruise line might arrange for a celebrity appearing on the ship to attend a cocktail reception, dinner, or a private question-and-answer session. In some cases, the charity gets part of what each person in the group pays and may earn free berths when booking a larger group. Then sell the free berths, too.

   Planning time: Six to twelve months

   People needs: Minimal. A few people are needed to sell cruises, publicize the trip, and coordinate with cruise staff.

   Costs: Minimal. Getting the word out is critical so paid ads may be worth the expense.

3. **Charter a boat for a day.** Rent out the whole ship for a day-long cruise to nowhere (cruise lines are especially happy to do these when launching a new ship or re-launching a refurbished one). Casino boats are good bets, too. Some regions are well-suited for famous-house cruises, in which passengers get a gander at celebrities' homes from the waterways.

   Planning time: Four to six months

   People needs: Minimal. The charity handles publicity and ticket sales.

   Costs: See budget worksheet in Chapter 2.

4. **A meal on board.** Cruise lines sometimes donate a meal to a charity to get potential customers on board. The charity brings in the people and the cruise line does the rest. This event is limited to the number of seats in the ship's dining room. People pay to attend. Add a raffle or mini-auction.

   Planning time: Three to five months

   People needs: Minimal. The charity handles publicity and ticket sales.

   Costs: Minimal. Publicity, invitations, and postage are the main expenses.

Dance

Without a meal to worry about, this can be an easy event to produce. All that's needed is a place to hold it, music (live or recorded), light refreshments, and some publicity. Tailor it to a particular crowd with the music. It could be '50s, '60s, country, rock, polka, hip hop, techno, big band, etc. Consider asking a radio station with a format compatible with the event to serve as a sponsor and, if possible, set up a live remote broadcast, which is likely to attract more people. Dances aren't generally large moneymakers but it's possible to boost profits with a program book, sponsors, raffles, and a mini-auction.

   Planning time: About three months

   People needs: Minimal to moderate. The group needs people to secure a site and equipment, handle decorations, find a DJ or band, publicize the event, and sell tickets.

   Costs: Virtually everything should be donated or underwritten or don't do it.

Designer Homes

This project is large and complex and requires seasoned fundraisers to produce successfully. It usually entails finding an empty house (either a new model or an older one now for sale), and several interior designers, each of whom decorates one room. Ticket prices are higher than for home tours (discussed a little later in the chapter). Designer homes take massive amounts of planning and coordination and can easily lose money. Increase profits by holding an opening night preview for VIPs, fashion shows, electronics/media show and demonstration night, garden and landscaping events, luncheons, auctions, raffles, a gift shop, and sessions with the designers.

Planning time: Six months to a year

People needs: High. Many people will be needed to coordinate with the designers, sell tickets, publicize the event, produce the side events, and staff every room of the house whenever it is open to the public.

Costs: Moderate. Designers cover the expenses of decorating the rooms and the labor involved. Sponsors should underwrite ads, promotions, printing, food, and other expenses.

Dine-Arounds

These can work three ways:

1. Arrange for three to five restaurants to each produce one course of a progressive meal in the restaurants. (They should be relatively close to one another to prevent long commutes.)

2. Ask several restaurants or well-known chefs to each produce one course at a variety of interesting homes. Participants travel from house to house for each course.

   Arrange for a tram, trolley, or bus to shuttle guests around.

3. Ask several restaurants to each stage a cooking demonstration and meal, preferably on different evenings. Participants may buy seats at one or more restaurants. Sometimes the establishments will donate a course or portion of the meal, leaving more of the admission for the charitable cause. Add to profits by holding a raffle in advance (sell raffle tickets while selling meal tickets) and possibly a mini-auction at each restaurant.

   Planning time: Two to four months

   People needs: Minimal. The group needs someone to handle publicity/advertising as well as a sales committee in which each member commits to sell 10 or more tickets or purchase the tickets themselves. Have another committee that sells raffle tickets at $10 each or $50 for a book of six tickets. Winners need not be present to win.

Costs: Liability insurance is essential.

Food Festivals

An event that celebrates a local specialty food—or a universally loved one—can be a fine reason for a festival. Obviously chocolate is top among those but countless communities hold festivals celebrating shrimp, garlic, strawberries, tomatoes, etc. It can be a group of restaurants competing against one another. Ask local restaurants to serve a signature entrée, appetizer, salad, or dessert. Restaurants can compete for honors by having a panel of judges vote on which had the best entree, best appetizer, best dessert, best booth display, etc. Have a people's choice award, too, allowing the public to vote for favorites as well. Charge each group or restaurant for the space, table, and electrical service. The charity handles publicity. People purchase tickets to be traded in for food. Add a raffle and program book that includes the layout of the event, thanks to each of the vendors, and ads (quarter-, half- and full-page) sold to participating vendors and anyone else who wants to support the cause.

Planning time: Three to six months

People needs: Moderate. Volunteers need to line up vendors, handle publicity, sell program book ads, gather raffle items, monitor the site the day of the event, and clean up afterwards.

Costs: Upfront costs include weather and liability insurance, site rental, set up and clean up, and specialized personnel, such as an electrician, plumber, fire department/emergency transport at the site throughout the event.

Fur Ball

Animal devotees love this event. A Washington, D.C. animal welfare group held a fur ball, in which those wearing fur were dogs that escorted their well-dressed (and presumably furless) human companions to a gourmet dinner, plus games such as bobbing for bones. This is basically a dinner event with a twist on the entertainment. All dogs must be leashed and have proof of current vaccinations. Add to profits with a doggy gift shop, raffle, and auction.

Planning time: Three months

People needs: Moderate. Volunteers must find a site, handle decorations, plan the meal and entertainment, and be on hand at the event to supervise and register guests.

Costs: Besides site rental and set-up and cleanup costs, plan on lots of security. Consider hiring professionals to supplement volunteers and both a veterinarian and medical professional (nurse, emergency medical technician, etc.) in case of mishaps.

Gay Bingo

This event won't work in all communities, but it's been enthusiastically received in larger cities, such as Philadelphia, Seattle, San Francisco, Dallas, Miami, and New York, where the games easily sell out. Seattle's games have taken place monthly since 1992. According to its Web site, upwards of 750 people attend each session. Admission is $20 and players must be 21 or older. Guest host and speakers appear. Bingo winners get $100 for each regular game. Drag queens (roller skates are optional) and celebrities serve as hostesses and number callers. Those who attend are encouraged to dress in appropriate costume for the evening's designated theme, which might be cowgirls, mistletoe, cops and robbers, Halloween, etc. In recent years, organizers have started selling dinners just prior to the games as well as beer and wine. Proceeds benefit the Lifelong AIDS Alliance.

Planning time: One month

People needs: Moderate to high. The event requires people to find the site, the entertainment, and the equipment and to be on the floor the night of the event.

Costs: Don't skimp on publicity. Hand out flyers, send e-mails, urge supporters to spread the word to friends, advertise in hip periodicals.

Haircuts

The first step is to get a local hair styling shop to commit a certain number of stylists and a specific amount of time to the charity. During that period, a percentage of sales goes to the charity. This one's particularly easy to produce.

Planning time: One month

People needs: Minimal. One or two people to handle publicity and someone at the salon to answer questions about the charity and, in the best of all possible worlds, recruit new volunteers. Someone should also ensure that food and beverages are available for the stylists and the customers. Get this underwritten whenever possible.

Costs: Minimal

Home Tours

Arrange for several private residences to hold open houses. Use historic homes or several houses in one interesting neighborhood. The biggest obstacle here is convincing homeowners to let scores of people traipse through their houses. People buy tickets to tour the homes. Add a program book and sell raffle tickets.

Planning time: Three to five months

People needs: High. There must be trustworthy workers in every room of each house, as well as people to handle publicity, and sales of tickets, raffle tickets, and program book ads.

Costs: Minimal. Buy plenty of liability insurance and make sure every home has lots of security.

Iron Chef

Have two or more chefs sign on to compete in a manner similar to that on the popular TV show. Each one gets a box with the same ingredients (they don't know what those are ahead of time) and they must create a dish with them in a specified amount of time. The public gets to watch the competition, then eat the results. Sell tickets to the event, add a raffle and program book.

Planning time: Two to five months

People needs: Moderate. The group needs people to sell tickets, get raffle items, sell program book ads, find a site, acquire all the equipment and supplies, serve food during the event, and clean up.

Costs: Moderate to high. Costs are lower if done in a restaurant where kitchen facilities are available; higher if the group has to bring everything in.

Jail

"Arrest" well-known local personalities then have them phone friends to post bail, the proceeds of which go to the charity. Advertise heavily so people know it's coming and make sure the people you arrest are amenable to it.

Planning time: Three months

People needs: Moderate to high. The event requires lots of drivers to pick up and return people and a bank of phones for bailout calls.

Costs: See budget worksheet in Chapter 2.

Mystery Night or Hunt

Participants solve a mystery, either by watching actors perform or by going on a hunt to gather clues and evidence themselves. There are professional companies that produce these and, unless someone in the group knows how to do it, hiring the experts usually pays off in this case. There are lots of site options: a shopping center, amusement park, empty building, estate, or farm would work well. Businesses might sponsor locations of items on the route, refreshment stands, and T-shirts. It's a good way to get people involved because a lot are needed to pull it off. This is an event that can grow over the years. Most only break even the first year.

Planning time: Three to six months

People needs: High if the group produces it on its own, moderate if a professional company handles it.

Costs: See budget worksheet in Chapter 2.

Non-Events

Send out cards inviting people to donate without attending an event. Donors will save money on clothing, gasoline, parking, and babysitters. This can be a great change of pace for a well-established group that has conducted the same sort of event for several years. New groups without a solid donor base should skip this one.

Planning time: Two months

People needs: Minimal. Volunteers send out invitations and collect donations.

Costs: Minimal

Pancake Breakfasts

This is an easy and inexpensive event to produce, but doesn't generally raise a lot of money. To add profit, hold a raffle, silent auction, or pass-the-basket. Send invitations by e-mail, phone, and flyers, signs at the fire station, and announcements in the news media.

Planning time: One or two months

People needs: Minimal to moderate, depending on the crowd. Workers cook, hold games, handle publicity, ticket sales, site procurement, and cleanup.

Costs: Minimal

Phone-A-Thon

Ask a local firm that has a phone bank or large room with lots of desks and phones if the charity can use it for a set period of time so volunteers can call people and solicit donations. This can raise a significant amount of money, especially from people who don't give on a regular basis. For this to be successful, gather a lot of volunteers to make calls—some during the day, others at night—and lots of phones. Award prizes to those who collect the most money.

Planning time: Three to six months

People needs: High. The more people making calls, the more money they will gather.

Costs: Office rental and meals for volunteers can be additional costs (unless the group secures a business to serve as sponsor).

Races

If it moves, it can race for money. Possibilities include boats, planes, cars, dogs, horses, turtles, crabs, skunks (de-scented please), rubber ducks, beds, cardboard crafts, etc. Weiner dog (dachshund) races are brief, funny, and very popular. Even the lowly cockroach has been known to race for charity.

Planning time: Six months

People needs: Moderate to high. Workers will need to arrange for the site, publicity, round up participants, and sell tickets.

Costs: Minimal

Sidewalk Sale

Sell candy, baked goods, rummage items, plants, or crafts. It's a good first-time event because it gets people involved and builds a following. Volunteers can procure items from home or collect them from garages and attics. This event requires a prime location (such as a busy shopping center), lots of people donating items, good promotion, and enough workers to handle the crowds on the day of the event. It won't raise a lot of money, but can be held regularly, serving as a solid source of revenue. An alternative is to have individuals list their items online at a service such as MissionFish, specifying that a set amount of each sale go to the charity. (See Chapter 8, Auctions and Other Profit Boosters.)

Planning time: One to two months

People needs: Moderate to high for a live event in which there must be setup and cleanup, collection of items, publicity, and someone to line up vendors and sellers. Minimal for online sales.

Costs: Budget money for permits.

Speakers

Bringing in a single well-known speaker, or a series of them, can result in big profits for relatively little effort. Either call upon someone with a connection to the group or consult a speakers' bureau, which helps match the right celebrity to the event, cause, and budget. Be sure to get written permission prior to the event when planning to video or audio tape a speaker.

Planning time: Depends on the group's choice of speakers and how much money would have to be raised for advance costs, but factor in at least three or four months. A speaker's availability can also dictate the date the event is held. Check with a speakers' bureau for possible speakers prior to setting a firm date for the event.

People needs: Moderate. People are needed to secure a location and speaker, sell tickets, round up sponsors, and publicize the event.

Costs: Local speakers generally cost very little or nothing, while nationally known speakers can command upwards of six figures.

Telethon

While the Muscular Dystrophy Association telethon with Jerry Lewis and periodic telethons on public television are by far the best known, lots of groups hold these with good results. They require a tremendous corps of volunteers, a bank of phones, lots of publicity, and a station willing to broadcast the program. If the group has limited funds, approach cable or community access channels, which are generally less expensive. This is an event for which it often pays to hire the professionals. A group can spend a lot of money staging a telethon before the first donation comes in.

Planning time: Six months to a year

People needs: High. This event calls for people to staff the phones, arrange for and guide speakers and guests, send pledge envelopes, and follow up.

Costs: Moderate to high (depending on how much is underwritten). The group will need a phone bank, TV time, advertising, and transportation.

Themed Meal

Pick an appealing site, stick to a budget, and get as much of the event's requirements donated as possible. Theme the meal around something such as a luau or country hoedown. If it fits the theme, add a fashion show. Tie in a raffle or gift shop that fits the theme.

Planning time: Four to six months

People needs: Moderate to high

Costs: See budget worksheet in Chapter 2.

Touring Shows

Plays, circuses, and other traveling shows afford great tie-in opportunities for nonprofits (see Exhibit 1.1). First, find a touring company coming to the area. Buy a block of tickets and sell them at a higher price, with the difference going to the charity.

Planning time: Six months

EXHIBIT 1.1   SOMETHING TO ROAR ABOUT WITH BROADWAY TICKET

Lion King Special Prize Program
Here's Your Chance to See Broadway's Sold-Out Sensation...
The Lion King

If you donate $100 or more you will be eligible to
win two (2) tickets to the *Lion King*
and join over 250 other supporters of the Jewish Community Centers
of Greater Philadelphia on Sunday, April 11 at 6:30 pm in New York City!

To purchase more chances, please call (215) 545-0153.

All proceeds benefit the programs and services offered by the JCCs of Greater Phila.
* Includes show only. Transportation not included.
Tickets must be reserved in name of user only. Non-transferable.

Please complete and return to the JCCs in the RSVP envelope.

Name _____

Address _____

City/State/Zip _____

Home Phone _____

Work Phone _____

People needs: Low to moderate. Volunteers are needed to line up the show, sell tickets, and arrange for tie-in activities.

Costs: See budget worksheet in Chapter 2.

Tournaments/Sporting Events

Tennis, golf, and car racing are among the most popular tournaments successfully used for fundraising. These require lots of manpower to find a site, line up sponsors, and handle publicity, not to mention the activities on the day of the event. The more sponsors, celebrities, and media time the group can secure, the more money it's likely to make. Advance expenses are apt to be greater than for many other events because of deposits required for the site, printing, and sponsor information packages.

Planning time: Four to six months

People needs: Moderate to high. Workers must sell tickets, find a site, arrange for refreshments, recruit competitors and sponsors, and publicize and staff the event.

Costs: If there will be VIP seating for major sponsors, add liquor, food, gifts, and other benefits to the budget.

THINKING IT THROUGH

Once there's a list of possible events, narrow it down to no more than three and complete the preliminary budgets for each (see Chapter 2, Money Matters). This should help narrow the field to one event that fits the group's goals and budget. Then assess, step by step, what it will take to produce:

- Determine where the event will be held.
- Reserve the date.
- Set ticket prices.
- Prepare tickets, invitations, and news releases.
- Draw up a schedule of tasks to be completed and deadlines.
- Based on that schedule, figure out how many people will be needed to produce it.
- Determine what committees are needed, how many people it will require to accomplish everything, and how many are available. Factor in that some people work full- or part-time, have children, and may have limited time to help. If the usual volunteers aren't able to handle it all, ask them to recruit others.

Factor in the time the manager will spend on developing and producing an event. For development officers and professional fundraisers, an event can eat up half of their working time over a six-month period. If there's an active committee with a competent chairperson, the manager's role should be reduced. Look at the big picture and decide if the manager can commit sufficient time and energy to this event. Sometimes it's better to skip the event. Instead, spend a few hours calling corporations or wealthy patrons and ask for large donations.

For those considering holding a different type of event than the group has staged previously—perhaps moving from several small events to a larger, more costly one—choose something that warrants a bigger ticket price, such as a dinner-dance/cruise or a concert with a big-name star.

Look at the types of events that are successful in the community. Even those that haven't been strictly fundraising events might be altered to raise money. If there isn't an existing event to which the group can tie its charitable fundraiser, consider holding an event that's already proven popular in the area.

Figure out the expenses, then add 10 percent for unexpected costs. Organizations that set standards for charities maintain that a properly run fundraiser should leave at least 60 percent for the charitable cause, with 40 percent or less devoted to expenses. There's no law that requires it, but public opinion can be just as effective an enforcer.

Remember what a hit the American Red Cross took after 9/11 when the head of the organization told Congress that of the $500 million the public donated to the charity's Liberty Fund for victims' families, about $200 million might be spent on other terror-related causes? Many donors were furious that every dollar wasn't going to the victims' families. The president of the Red Cross resigned. The charity ultimately changed its plans and pledged all the money to the families with an apology to donors. Nonetheless, it took a while for people to forgive the Red Cross and to resume giving.

That's a far more public meltdown than most groups are likely to experience. But it's vital that the charity be forthcoming with financial information. Make sure donors know that the charity understands, and adheres to, the industry's standards of ethics.

> **TIP** *Let contributors know exactly how much of what they pay would be considered a tax-deductible donation to the charity.*

TIME AND DATE

Proper timing is vital to success. A group can produce the best event of the social season, fashion it to the exact tastes of the target audience, and have lots of money and people to pull it off, but still fail if it isn't properly scheduled.

Most communities have some sort of social calendar or events schedule. (It's great to have someone in the group maintain a calendar on the computer so it can be updated regularly.) Check the Web sites of the local chamber of commerce as well as the convention and visitors' bureau and local newspapers and magazines.

Call the largest hotels and events venues (convention centers, arenas, etc.) and check with the director of sales or catering who will have bookings scheduled six months to a year in advance for major conventions and events.

Check such schedules to make sure the date the group is considering has not already been taken by a large event. Also ensure the date doesn't fall on a religious holiday. In college towns, make sure there are no big sports or social events that day.

When considering an outdoor event, check with weather experts for the possibility of bad weather. *The Farmer's Almanac* and the weather bureau are good sources. So is www.weatherunderground.com. The Web is a great source of historical weather information, enabling the curious to check weather on that date in previous years. Depending on the location, it seems obvious that it's unwise to schedule events during periods that are prone to bad weather, such as August through November during the height of Florida's hurricane season or February in snowy Minnesota. Of course, there are no guarantees no matter when the event takes place, but a little thought in advance can help lessen the chances of problems.

Consider other seasonal factors, too. An outdoor event held in Texas on a blazing September day isn't going to entice a big crowd. Schedule events during the most temperate months.

Some days of the week are better than others, depending on the event. Previews and other small events work best when held right after work on Tuesdays or Thursdays, before people go home. Schedule a Friday night event late enough that people have time to go home from work, change, and get to the event. On Sundays, set the time early enough that people will have time to get home and prepare for the coming workweek.

Where the event takes place counts, too. If the group expects 50 people to attend, don't rent a hall that holds 500. Similarly, a room that holds 50 won't work if 20 more people turn out. (Read more on this in Chapter 6, On Location.)

Before committing to take on a special event, make sure the group has the money and manpower it needs to make it fun and profitable. Read on for ways to ensure this.

And finally: Sometimes it's best not to have the event at all if the group can't muster the resources. First line up volunteers and sponsors. Then prepare a detailed budget that includes a worst-case scenario—how much could the organization afford to lose?—and determine how many people and how much sponsor support is needed. If the numbers don't add up, don't do it.

CHAPTER 2

Money Matters

Successful charitable events must aim for the same target that for-profit businesses do: to make money. And, like private-sector companies, charities must conduct thorough research to create a detailed plan before plunging in.

Creating a budget is a top priority. It helps organizers figure out if the charity can afford to hold the event, keeps costs controlled, and lets the event manager keep track of what's being spent where. Obviously, this isn't a final version, but make it as detailed as possible, including as many potential costs and sources of revenue as possible. The clearer the financial picture from the outset, the more likely the event will make the money it's designed to raise.

First, tally the upfront costs and manpower required to produce the proposed program. Some large-scale events can cost more than a charitable organization has on hand. Taking on a big, expensive event without sufficient upfront cash is extremely risky. Even if the event has the potential to raise a lot of money, not everything achieves its potential. There are always unexpected expenses. Perhaps tickets don't sell as well as anticipated. Suppose there's terrible weather at the time of the event that discourages people from attending?

Even an indoor event can lose attendance because of bad weather. The result: financial disaster. That's why crunching the numbers first is so important.

There are situations in which it is wiser not to have an event than to risk the group's financial security. If the first event on the list appears too expensive or problematic, go back to earlier possibilities and see if one of those might prove more manageable.

> **TIP** *Be generous when estimating money and manpower needs while figuring out the preliminary budget. Always get three estimates on each line item to ensure the most accurate idea of the going rate.*

So, how much can a charity afford to spend on an event? Once the working budget has been completed, and the cost determined, look at how much money the group has on hand.

If the group has $10,000 in the bank account and it costs $1,000 a month to keep the doors open, there's $6,000 available to spend on an event in the coming four months. That makes it easy to rule out a $60,000 event, unless major corporate sponsors come up with the remaining $54,000. (See Chapter 5, Other People's Money.)

If the group cannot afford to produce the event alone, approach other charitable concerns about splitting the costs and proceeds. Be very specific about which group does what and what each group's financial commitments and gains will be. Create a detailed agreement and sign it. Make sure it covers what the event is, where and when it will take place, how expenses will be paid, and how proceeds will be split.

> **TIP** *Before signing the contract, head to www.give.org and check out that potential partner with the Better Business Bureau's Wise Giving Alliance, which collects and distributes information about the finances and operating practices of hundreds of charities that solicit nationally or offer national or international services. It also has links to local BBBs for checking out smaller groups. For a second opinion, head to GuideStar (www.guidestar.org), which also keeps track of charities and how they operate.*

Whether the organization goes it alone or joins forces with another group, organizers should approach a fundraiser the way they might a home purchase: If they put too much money down on the front end, they are left with nothing to live on. Being special event–poor isn't any more desirable than being house-poor.

Following are some of the primary elements that should be included in a preliminary budget and some basic considerations for each.

LOCATION

OK, so the type of event has been chosen. Next, figure out where to hold it because the location plays a major role in analyzing what the event will cost. (See Chapter 6, On Location.)

Hotels

People often think hotels are among the most expensive options, but consider that a lot of the costs are included in the price. It's common practice for hotels to charge for the food and drinks, then throw in the ballroom as well as rooms for changing, meetings, and storage. In many cases, they might also offer the cocktail reception space and a terrace without extra charge. Not covered are items such as lighting, staging, decoration, and entertainment. Groups that decide to go that route, and are planning to have a large-scale stage show, should make sure the hotel's electrical and loading facilities can support it.

Convention hotels, which have conference facilities and good-sized ballrooms, are best suited for large-scale events and are more likely to be able to accommodate big stage shows. Naturally, they cost more, too.

Ask the hotel for a price sheet for additional services. Like gas stations, hotels directly across the street from each other can charge wildly different prices. While checking prices, let the management know how many rooms are needed for celebrities, volunteers, staff, and setup crews and the length of time they will be in use.

There's stiff competition among hotels in big cities. The bigger the event, the better the group's bargaining position. Those with a celebrity committed to appearing will have added clout and should lobby for everything they can get.

Prior to the event, the hotel will require the group to guarantee the number of people attending. Don't overestimate. That number is what the hotel staff uses to determine which ballroom would be most suitable, how much food to buy, and how much staff will be needed. Of course, the group pays accordingly.

> **TIP** *If the catering department won't discount the food prices, ask for free rooms instead. Many hotels provide free rooms for celebrities in exchange for photos of the stars at the hotel.*

Public Buildings

There are myriad public buildings that possess interesting spaces for special events. Think about what sort exist in the community. Spots such as city hall courtyards, museums, cultural halls, aquariums, airplane hangars, government buildings, warehouses, and buildings that haven't yet been occupied all have advantages and disadvantages. Charities can sometimes arrange for the use of such locales for little or no money. But free can still get expensive. Before committing, find out if there are restrictions on what can be done in that space. Some have no kitchens, glasses, dishes, or chairs. It may be up to the group to hire security guards and clean-up crews. Some places require users to not only pick up their own refuse, but to take it with them when they leave.

Homes of the Stars

Having an event at a celebrity's home can be a highly effective method of drawing public interest. People love getting a glimpse of how the stars live.

Houses of Worship

Churches and synagogues can prove ideal settings for a range of events. They generally have ample parking and large sanctuaries equipped with seating, and sound and light systems. Most have an area outside of the sanctuary that can accommodate a simple reception. If the event involves food, however, check to see if there are any restrictions as to what can be served or prepared there.

Other Indoor Options

Take a look at other large spaces, such as fraternal and service organization buildings. With some creative decorations and good food, it's possible to stage a top-drawer event without spending a fortune.

The Great Outdoors

Beaches and parks can work splendidly for special events because they are not only beautiful, they've got the goods, too: lots of parking and space, permitting several activities to take place at once. City or county parks, zoos, botanical gardens, beaches, water parks, a few cordoned-off blocks downtown, even the roofs of parking garages can work well, depending on the event and the group's ingenuity.

Check the costs of permitting, insurance, cleanup, security, emergency medical personnel, and other related fees before committing to an outdoor event. If alcohol is on the menu, make sure it's permitted at the space under consideration. Find out if the charity can charge admission to everyone who is there and if it's possible to exclude walk-ins from the street. It is sometimes possible to close a public venue, but it usually requires copious amounts of time, paperwork, and, like it or not, political clout.

LIGHTS AND SOUND

Lighting and sound may seem like secondary concerns, but if either one malfunctions, it can ruin an event. If no one can hear the speaker, or the ear-piercing screech of a maladjusted microphone drowns out a singer, or the actors appear as mere shadows on the stage, the people who have paid to attend will leave unhappy and may choose not to support future events.

The best way to lessen the odds of such mishaps is obvious: Hire professionals. Budget sufficient money to hire someone who does this for a living. Never mind that your nephew is a techno-geek who's a whiz with computers and musical components. This is not the place to pinch pennies. Find out exactly what equipment the performers require and shop around for a pro who can deliver it. Equipment requirements are among the many details outlined in a contract rider, which also spells out all of the other items and conditions a performer requires.

> **TIP** *Don't forget to ask whether the group qualifies for a discount because it's a charity.*

Pay careful attention to the audiovisual requirements for contracts involving celebrities and full-scale stage shows that are customarily produced in large venues. It's possible that the rider is designed for convention halls, arenas, and such, and might be too powerful for this event's location. Ask for one geared to the group's site specifications before signing the entertainment contract and rider. Consult with the tour manager early on. Discuss the size room the group is using and what equipment would work best.

FOOD AND CATERING

People who attend charity events will expect the food to taste and look good, but that doesn't mean the menu must include foie gras, caviar, and black truffles.

Food is one of the most costly aspects of producing an event and has the potential to devour every last dime in profits if not carefully and constantly monitored. If the budget is tight, go light on the meal and finish off with a lavish dessert spread. (See Chapter 7, Food, Glorious and Otherwise.)

Liquor can be every bit as expensive as food. Hotels may bill by the drink or the bottle and may also assess a corkage charge of as much as $15 a bottle, even if the wine was donated. The per-person liquor costs can easily equal those of a full meal.

Ideally, the cost of both food and liquor will be covered by an underwriter (see Chapter 5, Other People's Money). If it's not possible to get the entire food and beverage bill covered by underwriters, try asking several businesses to sponsor portions. If someone covers the cocktail hour, serve substantial hors d'oeuvres; then the meal that follows need not be as elaborate or costly.

When dealing with hotels, food costs are negotiable so send the group's best negotiator to handle this job. If the catering director quotes a price of $25 per person for stuffed sea bass topped with exotic mushrooms, suggest that he substitute button mushrooms and a less expensive fish to cut costs. Look for other ways to modify dishes to reduce expenses. Ask the caterer for suggestions, too. Because this is a charitable event, ask for a discount, with a promise to return the next year as an incentive. It doesn't always work, but does pay off sometimes.

> **TIP** *When discussing with the hotel or catering staff the number of people expected, be aware of what's known as a guarantee—a number the client must supply the hotel or caterer in order to determine how many people are attending and how much the establishment will charge. A week before the event, guarantee 20 percent fewer people than have paid. The group must provide a final guarantee 48 hours prior to the event. This one should be in writing. Be very careful with this. If the group guarantees 300 people but only 200 show up, it still pays for 300. Don't fret about guaranteeing fewer than actually show up. Caterers and hotel banquet staff routinely prepare 15 percent more food than the guarantee.*

If the event takes place somewhere other than a hotel, someone must supply all the equipment needed. Caterers do this for a price—generally 15 to 20 percent more than they pay to rent items such as chairs and tables. If there's someone in the organization who can handle this job, it can save a lot of money. Almost all communities have rental companies that can supply whatever the occasion requires. The person who takes on this job should find out exactly what the caterer plans to provide and what other items may be needed before renting anything.

FEEDING WORKERS

Volunteers generally work long hours, as do sound and lighting crews, entertainers, and members of the organization's staff. That means they need to eat. For paid personnel, such as the lighting and sound crews and entertainers, find out what they require. Some contracts specify precisely what's expected. For the staff and volunteers, sandwiches or pizzas and sodas are generally acceptable in addition to being quick and easy to serve and eat. Contact a fast-food delivery company to see if the management would be willing to provide the food in exchange for publicity at the event. Well in advance of the event, make sure the hotel will allow the group to bring in food from outside. Some try to prohibit this, but stand firm, especially if the group is spending a lot of money with the hotel.

> **TIP** *Include gratuities of 18 to 22 percent for the people who deliver and serve the food. The company they work for may provide food free of charge, but the workers still need to make a living.*

ENTERTAINMENT

While palatable food is vital to a successful event, so is making sure people have fun. The entertainment need not—and should not—be the most expensive, unless it's been donated or underwritten. Nonetheless, there will still be plenty of expenses and they rise along with the complexity of the program. Factor in money for sound, light, production costs, staging, and technical staff. When the event involves well-known celebrities, count on costs escalating on every front. (See Chapter 9, Reaching for the Stars.)

Include money for honoraria for entertainers, their transportation, hotel rooms, and meals. Celebrity contracts list the requirements. Add in some more for transportation, lodging, and meals for the core musicians.

> **TIP** *Some entertainers require certain brands of instrument, such as a Steinway piano or a Fender guitar. Check with local music stores to see if one is willing to loan the instrument in exchange for publicity.*

DECORATIONS

If the group plans to splurge on decorations—or needs to in order to make the venue presentable—this is an ideal opportunity to rustle up some underwriting and donations. The more, the better. If there's enough money in the budget, hire a party planner. It's likely that the result will be far more stylish. Planners usually have a collection of props and supplies the group can rent and they are likely to be pieces that would be prohibitively expensive for the charity to purchase for one-time use. A professional planner also relieves the charity's director and staff from handling the endless event-related tasks. When it comes to expense, a party planner may wind up being less costly than doing it without one and it's almost always less of a burden for the group.

> **TIP** *A party planner might discount or donate some of the work if the party will be a good advertising opportunity. Ask the planner to donate the work for all or part of one event in exchange for the promise of a future job that will be larger and more lucrative.*

SECURITY

More than ever, security is an important component of any event. Security personnel control crowds, protect the facility and those attending, and make sure crashers don't make it through the door. On an occasion when a guest has had too much to drink (and may also be a major contributor), it's preferable that uniformed security guards handle the situation rather than a tuxedo-clad committee member.

As with all things, get estimates first. Check to see if off-duty law enforcement officers are available for hire. They make the best security detail, if the local force permits it. If not, try private guard companies.

Have someone check the credentials of any limousine or shuttle drivers that will transport celebrities and other VIPs. Make sure they have good driving records and proper limo driver credentials. Also find out how long the company has been in business and check with the local Better Business Bureau to see if there are any unresolved complaints against the company.

INSURANCE

Many facilities require that the group purchase additional liability insurance to protect the site and the organization against injuries that may befall guests. These so-called umbrella policies also protect the group in case someone working on props or sets gets hurt. For outdoor events, weather insurance is a must.

GETTING GRAPHIC

Save-the-date postcards are usually the first exposure people have to an event (see Exhibit 2.1). They are sent out early in the social season so people can mark the event in their calendars. These need to be bright and eye-catching.

EXHIBIT 2.1 SAVE-THE-DATE POSTCARD— BASS MUSEUM OF ART

Shh... It's just the beginning.

Marisa Tomei, Sophia Loren, and Marcello Mastroianni have all saved the date! Have you?

Saturday, February 17, 1996
Friends of the Bass Museum presents the

American Gala Premiere
"Fellini: Costumes and Fashion"

at the Bass Museum of Art, 2121 Park Ave., Miami Beach

> **TIP** *There are easy ways to accomplish this inexpensively with a computer and basic software found at any office supply store. If possible, do flyers and posters the same way.*

Invitations can include corporate logos in return for the company paying all or part of the printing costs. Many large companies have their own contracts with printing firms and may be willing to print the charity's invitations as part of a larger run. (Some companies also have their own graphic artists who might be able to design the invitations, if needed.)

For occasions when the group opts to have a printer handle the job, make sure that all costs—paper, ink, graphic design, folding, and assembly (or whatever applies)—are included in the price. Make sure the printer can get the work done on time. And check before having the invitations produced that they won't require additional postage.

Don't under-order. Having a second, smaller run done is apt to cost as much or more than the initial printing. In addition to those needed to send to potential guests, add extras to send to the news media and to people on the committee members' personal mailing lists. (See Chapter 4, Committees and Commitments)

When it comes to budgeting, don't forget other printed matter: Media packets, posters, signs, tickets, certificates, plaques, books, and programs.

Shop around, getting at least three bids. Sometimes it's possible to barter with printers. For instance, the charity can give the printer credit in the programs and other printed materials and supply a certain number of tickets to the event in exchange for handling some of the printing the group can't manage on its office computers.

PUBLICITY

No matter how exquisite and compelling the event may be, there's little point in holding it if no one knows about it. Along with ticket sales, publicity is the key to pulling off a successful event. Don't just rely on the ticket sellers to handle this. Dealing well with the news media is critical to the cause.

Experienced event organizers can attest to how much impact this sort of exposure brings, especially in print media that readers can tear out and stick in their Day-timers or post on the refrigerator as a reminder. Effective promotion requires news releases, photographs, and advertising space. Many newspapers have discount rates for charities; others will list the group's event in community calendars at no cost.

Include money in the budget for ads, photos (and CDs), and related expenses. (For more on promotion, see Chapter 10, The Media and the Message.)

For a large-scale event, consider hiring a site publicist who gets paid a set fee for a specific set of tasks. That frees up the organization's director, staff, and volunteers to attend to other details. When hiring one, check prices and include it in the budget. (This is practical only for large groups with beefy budgets.)

Arrange for a photographer to document the process from the planning stages through the event itself. Often that's a volunteer armed with a digital camera. In that case, there's no cost. Generally, at least someone in the group is a shutterbug who will be happy to do this. If more than one person wants to serve, either designate one as the official photographer or specify which one shoots which part.

Photos go in the event notebook (a loose-leaf notebook that contains every detail of the event—more on that in Chapter 3, Who's In Charge?) and will be helpful with pre- and post-event publicity. If the group has to hire a photographer, account for it in the budget.

CARE AND FEEDING OF COMMITTEES

There may be occasions when the group will have to take top committee members out for a meal. Some restaurants will donate a luncheon for a small group of committee members, especially if they are socially prominent and are photographed there. (Send news releases afterward to area papers, making sure to mention the restaurant.) If the restaurateur won't donate the meal, and there's no company willing to sponsor it, budget money to cover this.

Depending on how well the designated negotiator does, a hotel may provide a certain number of planning meetings that include lunch or cake and coffee prior to the event. Some hotels allow groups to bring four to six people to taste-test the menu a month or so before the event. It's a nice perk and can stimulate key committee people to sell even more tickets.

FREE TICKETS

Give away as few tickets as possible. The fewer paid tickets, the less money comes in. Check with larger companies that buy blocks of tickets for executives and favored clients to see if they have any left over that they might be willing to donate to the cause and give those away if absolutely necessary. Make sure companies that do this get recognition.

POSTAGE

Include postage for publicity mailings as well as invitations. Add extra to cover correspondence with the news media (including press kits), key committee people, solicitation of corporations, and mailing out tickets. Reduce postage costs by sending some of that correspondence via e-mail. Just make sure that it doesn't land in someone's spam file.

Bulk first class mail rates may save money if the group is sending out at least 500 to 1,000 invitations, but it requires some training, has to be sorted by ZIP code, and can take longer to arrive. On the flip side, it can also provide the group with updated information on whether the recipient has moved, died, or left the country. Check the U.S. Postal Service's Web site, www.usps.com, for details.

> TIP *Those planning to send out a lot of items should consider hiring a mailing service to prepare them. They are faster and can prove more cost-effective than tying up office staff or burning out volunteers.*

SPECIALIZED COSTS

Because every event is different, each budget requires some special categories. A fashion show will include dressers, racks for clothing, makeup, hair styling, extensive staging, and runways. (See the list in the section "Setting Ticket Prices.")

At a food festival major costs include tenting and electrical generators. A guest speaker might require an honorarium. A big-name celebrity will necessitate extra security, transportation, and possibly a box office from which to sell tickets.

SPECIAL EVENT PLANNERS

There are many people who can help produce special events. Among them are:

- *Party planners.* Party planners come up with the theme, decorations, talent, music, and menu. Generally, they charge a fee and add a 10 to 25 percent markup on products and services. Keep in mind that their job is not to raise money and conserve cash. They are paid to create a smashing event. Be clear from the outset that this is a charity event and that they may make it just as fabulous as they want as long as they stick to the budget. Get the usual estimates and ask if they can discount or donate a portion of their services in exchange for promotional recognition.

- *Special events production firms.* Use one of these for large-scale events that call for outdoor staging, extensive lighting and sound equipment, gigantic projection screens, stadium seating, fireworks, crowd control, or all of the above.

- *Fundraising consultants.* These paid fundraisers look at the event from a financial standpoint, making sure the event will raise enough money and keeping expenses as low as possible. Consultants advise charities on innovative ways to increase attendance and how to entice companies to ante up underwriting and sponsorships. If they are good at their jobs, the extra money raised will more than offset the cost of hiring them. Look into their track records (insist on recommendations and check them out) before hiring one.

Fundraising consultants often maintain lists of affluent people and are likely to have established relationships with them. The consultants also have lists of companies that might be good sources of underwriting and support. In some cases, a consultant will oversee ordering invitations, devise the event's theme, and coordinate entertainment. They normally work for a straight consulting fee.

SETTING TICKET PRICES

Before deciding what to charge, have committee members question 100 or more people—yes, really—to see what they would be willing to pay for the type of event being considered. Check to see what other groups charge for comparable events. Make sure the price the group sets isn't more than people in the area are willing to pay. This kind of research is critical to creating a profitable event.

Once all the vendors' bids are in and the budget sheet is filled out, add 20 percent for a contingency fund. (Face it, expenses always crop up later.) Because the charity needs to reap a minimum of 60 percent of the money raised (more is better), double the amount estimated to cover expenses so there's a cushion.

Then look at the number of people group members think they can attract. This is a tricky step. If committees are properly structured, their obligations regarding ticket sales are clear, and they fulfill them, the number should be fairly accurate. (See Chapter 4, Committees and Commitments.) Take that number of people and divide it into the total expense. That gives the per-person amount the group must raise to cover the event's costs. Then it's time to come up with the final number. Here's how it works:

Estimate For Fashion Show/Luncheon

Number of guests: 300

Cost per person (food, postage, etc.): $50

Fashion show—underwritten: $0

Site rental—underwritten: $0

Total cost $50 × 300 people: $15,000

If the ticket price is $75, charity raises $22,500, netting $7,500

If the ticket price is $100, charity raises $30,000, netting $15,000

If the ticket price is $125, charity raises $37,500, netting $22,500

Keep in mind that worst-case scenario. The group may estimate 300 will attend, but maybe only 200 people buy tickets. Organizers may count on having most of the event underwritten, then find only half the expenses are covered. Before starting in on the event in earnest, the group's top leaders have to decide if the event is worth investing three to six months to produce for the amount likely to be raised.

DOUBLE CHECKING

To ensure that all costs are accounted for, take the now-completed budget sheet and mentally walk through the event, checking to see if the items needed for each step are covered.

- Where will it take place?
- Is there a parking fee? Valet or security?
- What will the entrance look like?
- Will props be needed? Stilt walkers? Klieg lights?
- Where will registration be held?
- How many tables and chairs will there be for registration?
- How many people are needed to handle it?
- Will they be volunteers or paid staff?
- What equipment will the staging areas require?

Visualize each part of the event to ensure that everything that costs money has been included in the budget (see Exhibit 2.2). Complete the budget carefully and accurately and it will provide a clear picture of where the charity stands financially and what it can safely take on. That's always a good way to start.

EXHIBIT 2.2   SAMPLE EVENT BUDGET WORKSHEET

EXPENSES	Cost
Space Rental	
Security	
Additional Site Costs	
Security deposit(s)	
Stage rental and set-up	
Dance floor rental & installation	
Tenting (outdoor events)	
Audio/Visual	
Special set-ups	
Workers/volunteers	
Insurance (Liability)	
Parking service or valet parking	

Food and Catering

Food purchases
Wine, beer, liquors
Bar set-up
Soft drinks, bottled water
Equipment rental
Gratuities (average 18%)
Staff meals
Tear-down costs

Entertainment

Live music
Hotel, travel, and transportation
Recorded music
Piano and instrument rental
Special set-up costs
Giant projector screen
Union musician fees or honoraria
Piano tuner

Auction Expenses

Decorations
Prop rentals
Flowers
Candles and candle holders
Lighting and other AV equipment
Special linens
Party designer
Party designer set-up crew

Total Expenses _____

INCOME	Ticket Price	Sales	Totals
Event ticket sales			$0.00
Sponsorship Levels			$0.00
Benefactors			$0.00
Patrons			$0.00
Sponsors			$0.00
Contributors			$0.00

	Price	Number of ticket sales	
Raffle ticket sales			$0.00
		Total Ticket Sales	$0.00
Cash Bar			$0.00

(continues)

EXHIBIT 2.2   CONTINUED

	Per-Ad revenue	Number of Ad Sales	
Program Book Ads			**$0.00**
Benefactors			$0.00
Patrons			$0.00
Sponsors			$0.00
Contributors			$0.00
Other advertisers			$0.00
		Total Projected Income	$0.00

SPECIAL EVENT UNDERWRITING

Possible saleable items	Value	Number of Sponsors	
Advertising—you can sell many event sponsorships			
Awards and plaques			$0.00
Dinner			$0.00
Food and service			$0.00
Liquor, wine, beer, and more			$0.00
Flowers and arrangements			$0.00
Party design			$0.00
Party favors			$0.00
Music			$0.00
Invitations			$0.00
Tickets			$0.00
Press packets			$0.00
Program book			$0.00
Signage			$0.00
Cocktail party			$0.00
Photographers			$0.00
Sound and light equipment			$0.00
Transportation and lodging			$0.00
		Total Underwriting	$0.00
		Total Income for Event	$0.00

CHAPTER 3

Who's In Charge?

Successful events depend upon the deft coordination of hundreds of tasks, large and small, all done correctly and on time. To make that happen requires a cool, competent person at the top capable of organizing the organizers.

That person is the event coordinator or manager. This individual recruits the workers required to get the job done, creates committees, assigns duties, ensures work happens on time, and keeps an eagle eye on the money. The charity's leaders should only appoint someone to this post who has a proven track record at producing events similar to those the group is contemplating.

If the organization has a fundraising director, that person often serves in this capacity. If the group has only an executive director, however, it's not likely that person would be able to devote the time required to coordinate everything and still fulfill obligations to other ongoing programs and projects. Most often, the executive director oversees the event manager, motivates volunteers, and plays a major role in securing underwriting and sponsorship contributions.

Hiring an event manager may be the most logical and cost-effective course for charities with few paid employees, rather than loading extra work on the staff members for several months or relying on several volunteers. Most groups couldn't operate without volunteers, but many have multiple obligations and so aren't always available as much—or exactly when—the group might need them.

Some groups are fortunate enough to have a cost-saving alternative: a seasoned volunteer who has successfully run similar events. Many volunteers produce events regularly and rival the pros in ability. Ask around. That person may already be a member of the organization. If there's no one within the group, look outside, scrutinizing social pages in newspapers and magazines to find movers and shakers in other organizations who might serve.

Some venues require that groups use their in-house event coordinator or a specific outside coordinator who is familiar with the facility. This is often the case at historical sites, country clubs, large-scale luxury resorts, and private or government properties. Whether the organization uses the facility's staff member or hires its own coordinator, don't underestimate the value of this key position.

PICKING AN EVENT COORDINATOR/MANAGER

Before an event is announced, key staff and executive board members should interview event manager candidates and select one. Here are some questions to ask:

- How many events has this person supervised before?
- What were they?
- Were they for publicity or fundraising purposes?
- How many people attended the publicity events?
- How much money did the fundraising events net?
- What was the percentage of profit vs. expenses?
- What were the three most costly event expenses?
- Could the person train staff or committee members to secure sponsors for the biggest ticket items?
- Did the manager create a realistic budget and stick to it?
- How much time can this person devote to an event?
- Would this person work from home or the charity's office?
- What kinds of leadership skills does this person have?
- How does the individual function under pressure?

Ask for the candidates' references and news clippings pertaining to previous events. Check all the references thoroughly. Ask lots of questions. Use a more delicate approach when asking a volunteer to serve in this capacity. Nonetheless, it is vital that the group thoroughly assess the person's abilities before awarding the job. All candidates must undergo interviews and supply references.

Make sure the person selected clearly understands the chain of command and that all decisions go through the executive staff and event chairpeople. Consider the candidates carefully, with a very critical eye. The consequences of picking the wrong coordinator/manager can prove costly.

Take the case of the International Red Cross Ball, a white tie-, tails-, and tiara- event founded by the late cereal heiress Marjorie Merriweather Post. For almost half a century, the event ranked among the biggest events of the winter social season for Palm Beach's old-money set. The opulent event attracted the town's aristocracy as well as diplomats and even a few European royals.

But in 2005, according to the *Wall Street Journal*, the Red Cross named Palm Beach newcomer Simon Fireman to chair the ball after he donated $750,000 to the local chapter. He moved the event from The Breakers, a renowned Palm Beach resort, back to Mar-a-Lago, Post's former home and now a private club owned by Donald Trump.

Although hundreds of Fireman's out-of-town friends attended the event and it raised a respectable $1.7 million, many of the town's long-time socialites boycotted the affair, instead attending a competing ball at The Breakers, the *Wall Street Journal* reports. It's anybody's guess whether those who attended the 2005 Red Cross Ball will return to support it in the coming years and whether it will win back its alienated long-time supporters.

The Event Manager's Job

This individual's primary tasks are fundraising, promotion, recruitment of volunteers, and overall management. An event manager can be especially helpful when charities are undertaking their first large events, such as an auction or concert.

Once on board, the event planner should meet with the executive director, potential event chairs, and members of the board of directors to present:

- A detailed timeline of the tasks to be accomplished, who is responsible for each one, and when they must be completed
- A list of vendors that will be used (including the bids gathered)
- A basic budget based on facts gathered in doing the task timeline

The group should review and approve all aspects of the event at this meeting and decide who will be authorized to write checks for approved pre-event expenditures. Another matter of business to decide: whether the group will open a special account for the event (a good idea) or funds will come from the charity's general fund account (a bad idea unless it's a very small, inexpensive event).

GETTING STARTED

Once the initial details are decided, the manager should start working with the individual vendors handling the food, décor, music, and printing. (See the event timeline checklist—Exhibit 3.1—at the end of this chapter.)

In the best of all possible worlds, it's now still a few months until the event, and it's a good time for the group to review all known costs, potential underwriting or sponsorship, as well as potential income from tickets, raffles, and/or a mini-auction. That's when the executive director, the board's financial chair, and the events manager should put together estimated best-and-worse-case scenario budgets. Based on those numbers and how much money the charity has that it can afford to lose, the group leaders must decide whether to move ahead with the event as planned, scale it down to reduce costs and risk, or cancel it.

Before committing to the event, an executive committee should review the financial information. This group might include the top people from the previous year's event, including the chairperson, co-chairperson, and perhaps the committee chairs who headed up food and decorations.

> **TIP** *When producing an event that takes place annually, appoint co-chairs for the event chair as well as the heads of each committee so the co-chair can head up that portion of the event the following year.*

A Vital Tool

Even though the computer now is the tool of choice when it comes to record keeping, maintaining an old-fashioned loose-leaf notebook can be helpful and adds another backup copy should a computer's hard drive melt down and the backup disk vanish or get destroyed. Keep a notebook with copies of everything related to the event. These records will also be maintained on the computer, but unless everyone involved has access to that computer, a centrally located paper copy provides easy reference when someone needs to check something. It's also an invaluable tool for those who will plan subsequent events, especially if the computer system changes in the meantime.

Label the dividers or computer folders as follows:

- Timeline and assignments
- Budget
- Sponsors
- Committees
- Correspondence
- Entertainment
- Invitations/printing
- Publicity
- Accommodations
- Travel/transportation
- Program book (if applicable)
- Auction and/or raffle (if applicable)
- Photography

- Registration (including tickets and seating)
- Schedule script (an hour-by-hour rundown of event and script for evening)
- Welcome kit
- Any other sections appropriate to the event

The front page of each section should consist of a checklist of tasks that must be carried out for that category. Behind the checklist go copies of correspondence, bids, contracts, agreement letters, etc. For easy reference, keep one notebook in the office and a duplicate at the home of the person in charge.

For backup and easy transfer, enter all of the information on the computer. Scan important documents or photos and download all entries onto a disk. Make hard copies and place them in the loose-leaf notebooks. Copy updated records onto a disk on the same day each week from start-up through completion of the post-event evaluation.

If the group uses Microsoft Outlook, members can employ the electronic calendar with pop-up reminders of dates related to specific tasks, as well as the times and locations of committee, budget, and other meetings.

Compile a list of all the key people, their home, work, and cell phones, e-mail addresses, fax numbers, and home and business addresses. Create the same sort of list of major vendors.

When ordering something, get a purchase order. Get copies of every signed contract. When someone agrees to donate something, send a letter saying the group will expect the item or money by a certain date. Put copies of everything in the books.

> **TIP** *Remove nothing from the notebooks. Make copies when something is needed away from the office.*

The advantages to a notebook system are that all details pertaining to the event are in one central, easily accessible place, and it is a vital reference for those who take over the following year. Keeping a detailed notebook not only helps the next set of chairpeople, but it can also prove useful to other groups that might need help with an event. After a while, the group will possess an invaluable library of reference materials.

Staying on Track

Create a timeline, listing every job that needs to be done, the date by which it is to be completed, and the person responsible for it. Set it up as follows:

DATE	TASK	PERSON

Place it in the front of the appropriate section of the notebook. Assign someone to each task, and send each one written confirmation of the specific assignment. If the organization has an office, put up a big poster board or sheets that list the tasks of each committee, then check the items off as they are done. If there is no central location or office, create multiple looseleaf sets and update and disseminate the information at least weekly via e-mail. Save important e-mails in computer file folders in My Documents.

While getting organized, clearly establish who has the final word in each area. This might be the event manager/coordinator, a knowledgeable chair, or the group's executive director.

It is essential to select one leader when dealing with groups composed of many powerful or influential people. The person who accepts the post must possess superior tact and finesse. It's not inconceivable that the event manager may have to work with an honorary chairman, the executive director, the city's highest-profile attorney, and the town mayor. All of these people are accustomed to being in charge, and all may expect to take command. It's up to the manager to make clear that just as they all are in charge of something elsewhere, they need to give the event manager the opportunity to do the job by taking charge of the event.

FINANCIAL CONTROL

Get bids for everything. The costs of sound, lights, and food can vary dramatically. Make sure bids are on comparable products and services. When dealing with services such as food or lighting, get recommendations from friends and associates, then gather at least three bids. Pick the most promising one, then try to negotiate a lower price.

> **TIP** *It may be easier to get a lower price if the group plans more than one event a year. The promise of future business is a powerful incentive for some vendors.*

About the Money

This may seem obvious but it's still worth saying: Collect all the money due. The best way to handle this is to collect it up front, but that isn't always possible. Big businesses, for instance, often take weeks to cut checks.

Collect as much money as possible before the day of the event. Then make sure that the registration staff knows who has yet to pay. Train them in how to encourage guests to pay without alienating them. For example, they might suggest that the person pay by check or credit card at the door, saying something like: "We're trying to keep our costs as low as possible so that the greatest amount of money can go to the charity, so it would be very helpful if we could have your payment tonight." If all else fails, have the guest sign a slip indicating he or she agrees to pay. Bill these people promptly after the event. It's customary to require a check when people reserve a block of seats. If they don't send one in, call and ask when it will be coming, or suggest they use a credit card.

Money Management

One person should oversee accounting and maintain the budget, take care of banking, purchasing, ticket sales, legal matters, and collections. It is better if it is someone other than the event manager, who must already keep track of countless details. If there's someone capable and conscientious within the group, give that person sole responsibility for tracking financial matters. Another alternative is to hire a competent bank executive or accountant, or convince one to become a committee member whose job will be to manage the money.

When planning a major event, one of the primary reasons to have a money manager is that many celebrities require payment by certified check on the night of the performance. Forget to bring that check and they will forget the show they had planned.

> **TIP** *Several days in advance, the event or money manager should pin the check to the outfit that person will wear to the event.*

Bank Accounts

For small-scale events, it is not worth the group's (or the bank's) time to open an account, but if the plan is to have several events or one larger one, it may pay off. Attempt to get the bank to sign on as a sponsor, providing free banking services to the group while the charity gives the bank a free ad in the event program book and a lovely banner at the event. If there's a board member who has a substantial account with the bank, have that individual ask the bank for an underwriting contribution along with the other benefits mentioned previously. The bank with which the charity already does business may provide free checking based on the group's account activity and monthly balances.

Keep a separate account for the event, if possible, so these funds and expenses will not get mixed into the charity's regular funds and expenses. Limit to one or two the number of people authorized to deposit or withdraw money. Have a debit card tied in with the event account. Only those authorized to draw on the account should know the access code. Know how many transactions are permitted before the bank charges for them.

Credit Cards

Credit cards are a must for any event. Because they are easy for people to use, accepting credit cards can boost sales. Accepting credit cards will cost the group 2 to 6 percent. The percentage generally is negotiable. The major cards have special programs for charities. National cards, such as Chase, MBNA, Juniper, etc., allow local bank branches to negotiate rates. Check with the bank with which the organization normally does business and call two or three others to see which has the best deal.

> **TIP** *At an auction, antique show, or "a-thon," where spur-of-the-moment purchasing is likely to occur, credit cards can sometimes double the amount made. At a ball or dinner, they probably won't make much difference unless there's a mini- or silent auction.*

The down side to credit cards is that they can be time-consuming because someone must check to see if a person's credit is good. The organization must buy the machines with which to process charge slips, and staff members need access to a conventional telephone line to use it. Sometimes the credit slips themselves cost money. And it can be embarrassing for donors if they have exceeded their credit limit and their cards get rejected.

Handling Ticket Sales

Tickets are money and should be handled as such. The best way to maintain control over tickets is to number them in two places—one on the stub the group keeps the other on the part the buyer keeps. Use these numbers for accounting. Make sure everyone selling tickets gets clear instructions on:

- How many tickets they must sell
- The deadline for selling them
- That they are responsible for those tickets even if they turn some over to others to sell
- Collecting money from people when they receive tickets

One way to simplify the process is to employ one of the many ticket management software programs available. Here are three examples:

- "The Raiser's Edge" (www.blackbaud.com) is a comprehensive fundraising program for nonprofits. It automates administrative processes, provides reports, and allows the addition of modules such as online fundraising, online ticket sales, and event management.
- ServiceU Corp. (www.serviceu.com) has online calendar software systems for churches, schools, and other organizations. Among the

products available is TicketU, online ticket software that manages reserved seat and general admission events.

- Auctionpay (www.auctionpay.com) has a suite of services that can be applied not only to auctions but other sorts of fundraising events. They provide for event management, online registration and donations, and an onsite payment process. There are planning guides, seminars, and consultants available to work with groups as well.

All committee members should develop lists of people they will approach. Give each member a support packet that includes handouts explaining the event and the charity. Encourage them to write down a brief pitch that explains what the event is and why someone should buy the ticket. If they have a place to post them, give them posters to put up. This can make a big difference in ticket sales.

The tickets themselves should include the name of the event, time, date, place, and cost per ticket, as well as the identifying number the group uses to account for each one.

> **TIP** *To help prevent counterfeiting, include a special design, logo, or trademark on the ticket that would be hard to copy, or select an unusual paper on which to print the tickets.*

Keep track of tickets by matching the person who is handling each block with a specific series of numbers. The previously mentioned computer software programs make this easy. But for small groups with tight budgets, use Excel spreadsheets on a secure computer. Expenses and income can be tracked and saved on an Excel spreadsheet in the event file in a computer. Always print them out and keep a hard copy in a notebook.

Boost sales by offering prizes to those who sell the most tickets. Many businesses will donate dinners, haircuts, facials, makeup lessons, or rounds of golf. For bigger events, consider offering a cruise or airline tickets. As another incentive, offer sales force members free tickets if they sell ten tickets to other people. (Make sure this is accounted for in the event expenses or find a business willing to sponsor the cost of these tickets.)

Give the sales force a list of contacts (chamber of commerce membership lists, Rotary, Yellow Pages listings, Web sites, etc.) and let the salespeople take the names of those at which they know someone personally. Make sure they contact all the large companies in town, as well as stock brokerage firms, banks, law offices, and hospitals. Either in person or via letter or e-mail, have them explain why they are involved in the organization and seek support for the group's fundraising efforts.

For large ticketed events, consider hiring a ticket service unless the group has the software and personnel to handle it. Usually there's only one ticket service in the area, such as Ticketmaster. The Yellow Pages usually list whatever ticket services operate in a given locale. For a negotiable percentage of sales (usually 1 to 3 percent), the company computerizes the tickets, sells them, and handles the bookkeeping and payment processing. Ask the ticket service to donate its services in trade for a sponsorship with a free ad in the group's program book, a hanging banner, or in brochures posted at the registration desk during the event. Every outlet maintains a Web-accessible list of events for which it sells tickets, so the charity's event gets added exposure there.

For an event that's likely to sell 2,000 or more tickets, a ticket service is usually worth the money. Because the committee people will have the names of people who should be sent invitations, arrange to retain that number of tickets so they can be sold to the people the committee members have contacted and the group won't have to pay the ticket service's surcharge. Again, the group could save that fee altogether by handling it with its own ticket management software program.

Make sure that everyone selling tickets knows when they must turn in the unsold ones. Keep track of ticket sales (and payments) as they progress to avoid a mistaken impression that the event is sold out when it isn't.

Ticket Accounting

Ticket sales can and should be handled on a computer using an event management program or, in the case of a small-scale event, an Excel spreadsheet. Those selling the tickets must report reservations and payments at least weekly so they can be added to the sales list. In the last two weeks before the event, reports should be made daily. This can be done easily via e-mail with the salesperson including the names, addresses, number of guests, and amounts paid. Excel spreadsheets work well, allowing the group to compare or track ticket sales with the event mailing list. This allows the group to know quickly who should be contacted or has not bought tickets.

> **TIP** *When recording the names of ticket buyers, make a note of who made the solicitation and/or sale.*

Keep a ticket ledger separate from the event notebooks, with copies in the charity office or the event-planning headquarters. The ledger should list each ticket number and who is responsible for it. These can be printouts from a ticket tracking software program.

On the night of the event, collect the stubs from all the tickets. Later match them to the numbers recorded in the ledger. This makes it easy to see how many people actually showed up and reconcile the numbers with the amount of money collected.

> **TIP** *Ticket sellers should get cash first, count it carefully, then deliver the ticket.*

Free Tickets

Inevitably, numerous tickets get handed out to people who don't pay for them—local bigwigs, the news media, etc. Try to get someone to underwrite them. Give the businesses or individuals who underwrite or sponsor tickets to be given away credit on signage at tables and in the program book, and create a media table, with the underwriters' names prominently displayed.

> **TIP** *Ever more newspapers are prohibiting reporters from accepting free tickets. Either the person pays (and usually is reimbursed by the paper) or cannot attend.*

Papering the House

To make the event look sold out when it isn't, groups sometimes "paper the house"—give out free tickets to civic organizations, police groups, retirement homes, students, and others who might not otherwise be able to attend, thus exposing more people to the cause. This is an alternative if ticket sellers have exhausted all avenues of selling tickets and organizers believe they have made all the money they are going to make on tickets. Use a giveaway only for events at which it doesn't cost the group any more to fill up the seats, such as a show. Never do this for sit-down meals. Sometimes it's possible to get a mention in the local newspaper about how the group donated seats to another deserving charity or group.

EXHIBIT 3.1 EVENT TIMELINE

Tasks needed 6 to 12 months prior to event	Assigned To	Date Assigned	Date Needed	Date Completed
Define purpose				
Choose event				
Explore potential sites				
Research/recruit chair				
Research/hire event manager				
Assess manpower				
Form committees				
Select venue				
Estimate costs/seek bids (for site charges, food, lights, equipment)				
Seek music referrals/auditions				
Bid music and entertainment				
Bid decorating costs				
Bid printing costs				
Seek bids on other needs				
Arrange photography (for advance shots and event)				

EXHIBIT 3.1   CONTINUED

Tasks needed 6 to 12 months prior to event	Assigned To	Date Assigned	Date Needed	Date Completed
Select graphic artist to design invitation				
Secure permits/insurance				
Draft budgets				
Appoint budget manager				
Research/name honorees and VIPs				
Compile mailing list				
Compile e-mail list				
Estimate total number of guests				
Check date for conflicts and finalize				
Get written contracts for food, talent, site, etc.				
Assess available upfront funding				
Procure alternate site (if event is outdoors)				
Plan pre-party event				
Invite/confirm VIPs and honorees				
Identify items and possible sources for underwriting				
Order "Hold-the-Date" cards				
Set publicity schedule				
Compile media list				
Draft news release, calendar listings, e-mail alerts				
Set schedule for release of media info, e-mail alerts				
Research special permits needs, insurance, etc.				
Get bios/info on VIPs and others				

EXHIBIT 3.1 CONTINUED

Tasks needed 3 to 6 months prior to event	Assigned To	Date Assigned	Date Needed	Date Completed
Set schedule for committee meetings				
Compile list for possible sponsors/underwriters				
Send formal requests for underwriting/funding to major donors/corporations/sponsors				
Review designs for invitation, posters, return cards, e-mails				
Prepare final copy for previous items				
Prepare final copy for tickets, parking permits, etc.				
Order invitations, posters, etc.				
Finish mailing lists for invitations, posters, and e-mails				
Obtain lists of potential attendees from honorees/VIPs				
Arrange radio/TV sponsor, promos, PSAs				
Set menu				
Get written reply on celebrity participation/specific needs				
Finalize sound/lighting contract				
Select and order awards and trophies				
Tasks needed 2 months prior to event	**Assigned To**	**Date Assigned**	**Date Needed**	**Date Completed**
Address and stuff invitations, including personal notes				
Mail invitations				
Hold underwriting/preview party coinciding with mailing of invitations; invite the media				

EXHIBIT 3.1 CONTINUED

Tasks needed 2 months prior to event	Assigned To	Date Assigned	Date Needed	Date Completed
Distribute posters				
Finalize transportation, accommodations for VIPs, honorees				
Finalize contracts for decorations, rentals				
Confirm radio/TV presence				
Send press releases for celebs, VIPs, and honorees				
Get sponsors' corporate logos				
Determine number and location of needed signage				
All chairpersons review plans				
Hold event walk-through with committee chairs, staff, vendors				
Review and revise budget				
Review task assignments				
Start phone work for table sponsorships (corporate, VIP)				
Tasks needed 1 month prior to event	**Assigned To**	**Date Assigned**	**Date Needed**	**Date Completed**
Phone follow-up on tickets				
Place newspaper ads				
Contact news media for stories, announcements, and calendar listings				
Compile contents list for VIP welcome kits				
Confirm host/registration staff and schedule				
Assign tables/seats				
Give caterer guest estimate				

EXHIBIT 3.1 CONTINUED

Tasks needed 2 weeks prior to event	Assigned To	Date Assigned	Date Needed	Date Completed
Continue phone follow-up for ticket/table sales				
Assign seats/head table, and speaker's platform				
Arrange to meet VIPs at train/airport/hotel				
Confirm all transportation (airline, bus, train, limo, car)				
Confirm lodging				
Prepare transportation and lodging checklists (flight number, airline, who meets flight, etc.)				
Confirm security for VIPs				
Prepare welcome packets for VIPs/chairs/key staff				
Schedule deliveries of equipment, rentals				
Meet with committee chairs/vendors/staff				
Confirm setup time with site				
Finalize plans with party designer				
Meet with chair and staff for finalizing plans				
Tasks needed 1 week prior to event	**Assigned To**	**Date Assigned**	**Date Needed**	**Date Completed**
Finish phone follow-ups for sales				
Confirm number attending				
Finish seating assignments				
Hold training session with volunteers/finalize assignments				

EXHIBIT 3.1   CONTINUED

Tasks needed 1 week prior to event	Assigned To	Date Assigned	Date Needed	Date Completed
Name three volunteers to assist with emergencies				
Finalize registration staff				
Distribute seating chart table assignments to host				
Schedule return of rented/loaned equipment				
Reconfirm delivery time with vendors				
Reconfirm event site, hotel rooms, and transportation				
Finalize the catering guarantee				
Finalize snacks/meals for confirmed volunteers				
Deliver final scripts				
Follow-up calls to news media for both advance and event				
Distribute more posters				
Hold final walk-through at site				
Schedule rehearsals/volunteer assignments for event				
Establish amount of petty cash needed for tips, emergencies				
Check or clean outfit for event				
Pin cashier's check for celebrity, special permits, etc. on outfit being worn to event				
Day before event	Assigned To	Date Assigned	Date Needed	Date Completed
Lay out clothes for event				
Make sure all petty cash and checks are ready				

EXHIBIT 3.1 CONTINUED

Event day	Assigned To	Date Assigned	Date Needed	Date Completed
Arrive early to unpack and inventory supplies, etc.				
Check for VIPs in place with scripts				
Reconfirm snack and meal schedule for volunteers				
Check with volunteers to ensure all tasks are covered				
Set up registration area				
Check sound/light equipment and staging before rehearsal				
Hold rehearsal				
Review details with caterer				
Make final calls and faxes				

CHAPTER 4

Committees and Commitments

While the money-hungry souls of charity directors may thrill to see a star-studded list of movers and shakers serving as honorary committee members, remember that honor isn't everything.

Appoint anyone who might add some panache and allure to the event, but never forget that success depends on working committees composed of motivated individuals who put everything together and bring in supporters.

Think of committees in fishing terms: The honorary committee serves as the tasty bait; the working committees act as the rod, reel, and hook. Organized and supervised properly, it's a winning combination, especially when honorary committee members take an active role.

THE RECRUITING PROCESS

Recruiting effective, motivated committee members to serve as volunteers is critical to an event's success. Devote the same energy to recruiting volunteers as to acquiring sponsors. These are the people who will invest sweat equity, an immeasurable but invaluable commodity.

When going about the business of recruiting, consider that people are motivated by different things. Always use an upbeat and enthusiastic approach when trying to enlist help. Explain what the charity does and how it makes a difference.

As a result, some people will decide they want to get involved because the charity has helped loved ones or the cause affects them personally. Some will be motivated to help others, giving back to their community in some way. Some seek recognition or are looking to broaden their circle of acquaintances. Others may feel obligated to someone in the group and want to repay a previous kindness. Some are pure altruists—doing it just for the satisfaction of helping mankind. Whatever the case, the group may reap rewards just because someone thought to ask.

Ask all friends, family members, and acquaintances to volunteer. Ask them to ask everyone they know to join in, too. Make sure board members do their share of networking. Persistence is the key to rounding up a competent, involved team.

Honorary committee members generally are upper-income people with significant social prominence, whereas working committee members generally come from a broader spectrum of the socio-economic scale.

Every committee member should get a formal invitation to serve. The letter should clearly state the recipient's responsibilities: "As a member of the committee, you are expected to put together a table of ten friends," or "purchase ten tickets," or "acquire and install all decorations," or whatever the task. Clearly spell out all duties. Include in the letter an estimate of how much time the volunteer will be expected to put in and how many meetings are planned (as well as the dates and times, if possible). Exhibit 4.1 shows a sample invitation letter.

At the committee's first meeting, every member should receive a kit that provides information that familiarizes them with both the event and the organization it benefits. Include the group's mission statement, copies of any recent news stories, the latest charity brochure, and newsletter. There should be a fact sheet about the event, a list of all the committees and their members, including contact information and what organizations they represent (if applicable). Other enclosures might include a contract for program book ads, a form on which they can keep track of tickets sold and to whom, and the tickets themselves (which have been numbered and recorded on a master list).

Each committee must function as a cohesive group with two purposes: making the event financially successful while making it memorable enough that people will want to attend again. This is a difficult balance to achieve. It's far more likely to happen if the group appoints a competent event manager to keep track of all the committees and their responsibilities, someone who keeps an eye on the big picture (as explained in Chapter 3, Who's In Charge?). The manager is, in essence, the CEO of the event.

EXHIBIT 4.1   SAMPLE COMMITTEE
INVITATION LETTER

August 16, 2006

Dear Marissa:

On Sunday, Nov. 12, 2006, The Women's Corps for Cancer Research will hold its fifth annual "WOMEN WHO LEAD" recognition and awards dinner. The event will be held at the new Mandarin Orange Hotel, at the Time-Warner Center, in New York City. We are honored to invite you to join the committee that will plan and host this prestigious event.

We are delighted to be able to hold this annual event with a pre-event reception for the honorees, their special guests, and our committee members in the center's atrium, followed by the awards ceremony and a light supper in the hotel's main ballroom.

During the past five years, we have strived to honor not only individuals in the entertainment industry, but also women who have made significant contributions toward improving diagnosis and treatment of cancer.

This year we will honor Mrs. Cornelius Smith and Ms. Sarah Cohen for their extraordinary work in raising funds, public awareness, governmental and public support to quick-track promising new clinical approaches to treating cancer.

We are proud to announce that awards will also be presented to Sen. Hillary Rodham Clinton, Maya Angelou, and Katie Couric. The evening's award ceremony host will be CNN news anchor Anderson Cooper.

We ask you to join our committee with the understanding that you are making a commitment to help organize and promote this special evening and also work with the other committee members to secure underwriting for all aspects of the event.

In order to maximize the funds raised from the event that go directly to cancer research, we also ask for your commitment to buy or put together groups of friends and colleagues to purchase tickets or tables. Our staff will be available, by appointment, to help you send invitations to individuals on lists that you provide.

This internationally recognized evening raises significant funds for The Women's Corps for Cancer Research. The Women's Corps is quite proud that its total operational costs are less than 12 percent annually, so that the remaining 88 percent support cancer research.

Women like you are helping to make positive changes in our world by your active participation in cause-related events. Your participation is very important to us and will greatly assist in our fundraising that supports cutting-edge treatments and continued research. Thank you in advance for agreeing to be actively involved and serving on this event committee.

When planning a dinner, for example, each committee member commits to buying one table and selling one. If the group plans a 300-person event, each of 15 committee members buys a ten-seat table and sells another. The event quickly sells out. Even if a few people don't honor their commitments, there are only a handful of tickets left to sell.

MOTIVATING THE TROOPS

Adequate staffing is essential to an event's success. Assess the resources that exist among the board, paid staff, and key volunteers. Then figure out where there are gaps and go after the people needed to do those jobs.

> **TIP** *When asking someone to volunteer, do it in person. A personal appeal is a powerful motivator.*

A few ways to find and recruit the high-caliber people needed include:

- Reading social columns of local newspapers to determine who the movers and shakers are, then seeking them out.

- Seeking involvement from upper-level managers of large corporations or businesses.

- Looking for new businesses that might want to draw attention to themselves. Sometimes the principals will sign on.

- Asking key volunteers to bring in friends, business associates, and acquaintances.

- Appealing to large service companies, such as accounting and law firms, banks, and stock brokerages for potential committee members. These people have large client bases to which they may be able to sell tickets.

- Seeking involvement by other service organizations whose major goals are fundraising, such as the Junior League, Kiwanis, Rotary, Optimists, and ZONTA. These organizations are particularly useful in helping to publicize events and making follow-up phone calls.

- Checking high schools and area colleges (don't forget fraternities and sororities) that might have service groups that would work for the charity. This is a great way to get young people involved.

Honorary Committees

Honorary committees traditionally consist of socially prominent people—business leaders, religious leaders, politicians, socialites, celebrities—through whose participation the group can attract more support for the cause. Generally, the honorary chairperson's role consists of lending an influential name to the event. Honoring a prominent chairperson at the event encourages the honoree to invite business associates and friends.

Committees of One

If the charity's karma is good, it may happen upon one well-heeled and high-powered individual who needs no committees and will host an event for the organization, covering all the planning and expenses. In some rare and wonderful instances, this person is a widely known celebrity who offers to open his lavish estate, engage his favorite caterer, and throw a party to raise money for the cause.

That's what Sylvester Stallone did for the United Way of Dade County in Miami, Florida. Not only did he open his bayfront home in Coconut Grove, he also brought in musician Emilio Estefan and *Miami Herald* publisher David Lawrence to co-host this exclusive sit-down banquet and auction, which took place waterside. The actor limited attendance to 400 people who had pledged major contributions to the charity. What few tickets remained went to those who donated at least $2,500 per couple to United Way.

Needless to say, the event was a sell-out and a highly successful fundraiser, netting $200,000 for the charity, according to the *Miami Herald*.

WORKING COMMITTEES

Working committees do just what the name implies: They work closely with the charity's paid staff to produce the event for the amount budgeted. These committees often include the following.

Decorations

This group comes up with the look of the event, and deals with vendors or a party planner to create that look. Members take care of renting tables and chairs, if necessary, and obtaining door prizes. (If the group plans to give away lots of door prizes, there should be a separate committee to handle this.) This team also handles the assembling and dispensing of giveaway bags guests receive. Every member sells tickets.

Entertainment

This committee coordinates music or whatever entertainment is planned, working closely with the event manager to acquire appropriate talent for the amount budgeted. The event coordinator/manager usually negotiates the contracts with entertainers. All committee members sell tickets.

> **TIP** *If possible, ask either an attorney who is familiar with entertainment contracts or a local entertainment promoter to serve on this committee. That person can be responsible for reviewing the nuts and bolts of the contract and rider for entertainment.*

Table or Ticket Sales

Although all committee members are expected to sell tickets, that's all this group does. The more people on this committee, the greater sales are likely to be.

Members of this group usually commit to buying a certain number of tickets each and selling a matching number. They formulate the list of people to whom invitations or notices will be mailed, and they solicit block purchases from corporations and individuals. A subgroup, the phone committee, does the follow-up phone calls to get people signed up.

For a large-scale event, manpower is always a concern. To help spread workers further, consider using a ticket service agency. (See Chapter 3, Who's In Charge?.) These services have massive exposure through Web sites and monthly newsletters. They also run outlets in many places and will handle the sales. As long as the event will require the sale of at least 2,500 tickets, using a ticket service can be well worth the cost. It can also reduce the number of people needed for the ticket sales committee and will simplify bookkeeping.

Publicity

If the organization is large enough to have paid staff members, they normally handle publicity. But in some cases, a small cadre of volunteers can be responsible for writing news releases, researching who to send them to, sending them out, and making follow-up calls. The same person who sends out the releases should do the follow-up phone calls.

Only one person should work with each media outlet. Newspaper, TV, and radio people get bombarded with requests for coverage and are apt to become hostile if they must deal with several people calling about the same event.

On the day of the event, one or two members of this committee usually serve as media liaison. All members sell tickets.

Invitations

This can be either a committee unto itself or a subgroup of the decorations committee. This group compiles the e-mail list and the mailing list or provides invitations to people who have their own lists but don't want to release them. The committee chairman needs to follow up to make sure everyone who does personal mailings gets them out, and that all the invitations are mailed in a timely manner.

> **TIP** *Appoint at least one highly computer-literate person to this group to get the message out via the Internet and e-mail.*

Because some people are reluctant to release the addresses and phone numbers of those to whom they mail invitations, ask the chairpeople for copies of the names only in order to merge them with the master list and eliminate duplicates. Once all the envelopes have been addressed, arrange them alphabetically or by ZIP code and again check for duplicates. Do this before putting postage on the envelopes.

This committee also decides on the design, format, and content of the invitations; creates them using a computer program; or negotiates and co-ordinates with the graphic artist and printer to design and produce them. Members also proofread the invitation before it is sent out. All sell tickets.

Food

This committee develops the menu, based on the event's theme and budget. Members coordinate with the hotel, caterer, or volunteers who will prepare the food. If volunteers are purchasing and preparing the food, this may be a subgroup of the food preparation committee. Either someone from this committee or the event coordinator/manager negotiates the contract with a hotel or caterer. If additional kitchen equipment is needed, this group sees that it is ordered, delivered, and returned. All members sell tickets.

Registration and Check-In

Registration and the work of the committee in charge of it start long before the day of the event. One person—the chairperson, a secretary, or volunteer—should be in charge of keeping track of who is coming. Other members of this committee make sure the proper equipment—computers, tables, chairs, etc.—gets to the registration site. They determine what to give people as they check in—a program, table assignment card, etc. They handle check-in on the day of the event. All members sell tickets.

At least one computer-savvy member is needed to set up and train other members to use computer software now available, such as Seating Arrangement (www.seatingarrangement.com) and another offered by The Raiser's Edge (www.blackbaud.com). Today's software programs significantly simplify registration and seating. See Chapter 13, Tools of the Trade, for a list of computer resources or search online for "Event Seating Software."

Set up a registration system, preferably on a computer on which it can be quickly and easily updated. Even so, keep a detailed, running alphabetical list of who plans to attend. On this same list, track whether the person has paid.

For example, if the event is a sit-down dinner, every name should have a table number listed with it. Make a list with the number of tables planned and eight spaces for each table. Fill in the names of those who will sit at each table. For each person attending the dinner, the entry should list with whom they wish to sit and their food preferences.

While the actual registration is done by staff or volunteers, the seating plan is formed by the chairperson and a few others. First, they should walk the room and decide how the tables will be set up. (In the case of an outdoor event such as a crafts show, someone must decide the lineup of vendors the same way.)

Although many members of the registration team may be experienced at it, it never hurts to practice before the guests arrive. If there's time, conduct a run-through at the event site. If that's not possible, gather everyone for a practice session at someone's home or at the office a few days before the event. Assign some workers to play the parts of impatient guests, or those with registration problems. Teach the staff how to handle these situations. Also teach workers how to tactfully ask for money from those who have not paid. They should politely ask for a check or credit card (if the group accepts them) and, if the guest has neither, ask the person to sign a pledge slip to pay later.

Make sure everyone who is working on the event has a cell phone and all know how to reach everyone else. Taking the time to make sure everyone has everyone else's phone numbers readily available will speed communication and make things flow more smoothly.

Program Book

This group decides how many pages the book will be and what it will look like. Members sell ads in the book, write whatever copy is needed, supervise printing, collect money from advertisers, and make sure the books get distributed. This committee should be large. As with tickets, the more people involved, the more ads get sold. All members sell tickets.

Special Committees

Many events require additional committees. For example, an auction must have an acquisitions committee. An arts and crafts or antique show calls for a committee to coordinate vendors and booths. Consult the checklist to see if there are duties on it that do not fit into any of the other committees, and then form the special committees to attend to them.

Depending on the size of the volunteer staff and the nature of the event, the number of committees needed may be as few as two or as many as ten.

A member of the working committee should meet regularly with members of honorary committees. Though this is time-consuming, it is time worth investing. Regular contact allows the working committee repeated access to honorary committee members' contacts; in other words, the people with the most money. The more people approached to buy tickets or underwrite costs, the more money the group makes.

Follow these guidelines to make sure working committees are consistently productive:

- The overall chair or staff person who supervises the running of the show divides the duties of an event among the committees and makes sure that each group knows exactly what is expected.

- The overall supervisor designates the chair of each committee in writing, spelling out duties, goals, and budgets. Pick chairpeople who are the most tactful, organized, and able to hold productive, concise meetings. They must also be willing to finish tasks that committee members fail to complete.

- Meetings are necessary, but do not meet simply for the sake of doing so. There should be a purpose to each gathering. Meetings should start and end on time, and last no longer than one hour. Thank all committee members at every meeting. When possible, take care of minor matters by phone, fax, or e-mail. Because most people have limited time to spare, committees should gather only to report on progress and decide what is to be done next.

- The committee chairpeople should meet at least twice the month before the event so everyone gets an overview of what is happening and can share ideas.

- All committee chairpeople should report monthly to the event coordinator.

It's vital that all committees come under the direction of a single coordinator. Committees left to their own devices can create big problems and seriously damage the bottom line.

> **TIP** *Make it absolutely clear to all committee chairpeople that the charity's authorized representative is the only one permitted to make financial commitments.*

A case in point: At a gala dinner for 600 in Miami, the event planner was surprised to find that the menu had been changed from the agreed-upon chicken dish to a lobster-and-steak dinner. Obviously, there was a big difference in price. The chairperson of the food committee said a local supermarket chain had offered to donate the filet mignons so the chairperson felt the group could afford the change. However, she failed to note that the addition of the lobster increased expenses by $6 a person, a total of $3,600.

> **TIP** *Make sure all vendors know who is authorized to make financial commitments for the event.*

Volunteer Retention

While it is important for everyone involved to focus on producing the event and making a profit while doing that, it's up to the leaders to make sure that workers, especially volunteers, know that their efforts are appreciated. Some TLC for volunteers goes a long way toward motivating them to work hard for the event and lend a hand again at future events.

The event coordinator should make sure that all committee chairpeople thank their team members at every meeting. Soon after the event has taken place, each volunteer should receive a thank-you letter and a small gift of appreciation, such as a plant or some memento that's related to the event.

When the budget allows, hold an appreciation lunch or dinner for all those who worked hard to make it a success.

Regal Recognition

Although there's no group that could spend as lavishly as she does, Oprah Winfrey set a diamond-studded example of how to say thank you with her legendary Legends Ball in 2005. The people she sought to pay tribute to were African-American women who inspired her: 25 legends, such as Coretta Scott King, Maya Angelou, and Tina Turner, assisted by 42 "young'uns," including Halle Berry, Mariah Carey, and Angela Bassett.

The event spanned three days and included a Friday luncheon at Winfrey's 42-acre estate in Montecito, Calif., then moved to the Bacara Resort & Spa in Santa Barbara for Saturday's gala ball, then returned to her home on Sunday for a gospel brunch. At the lunch, the younger achievers paid tribute to the legends with a reading of the poem "We Speak Your Name," by Pearl Cleage, calling out the name of each of the honorees.

The guest list for the gala included Quincy Jones, John Travolta and Kelly Preston, Barbra Streisand, and Senator Barack Obama.

In addition to the elaborate meals and the gala ball, Winfrey gave each of the honorees tokens by which to remember the event: the legends received 6-carat diamond teardrop earrings while the younger women received 10-carat black-and-white diamond hoops. "This was more than fabulous," Winfrey told *People* magazine. "It defined the word 'extraordinary.'"

Obviously, a nonprofit organization could not stage such an elaborate and costly affair. Nor should it, even if someone with deep pockets offers to foot the bill. (The exception to that rule might be Winfrey, considering that she also donates millions to charities each year.) That money would be far better spent on the charity's work. But Winfrey sets an example worth emulating on a more down-to-earth scale.

CHAPTER 5

Other People's Money

While gifts from individuals represent the largest segment of philanthropic giving, corporate sponsors can boost a charity's profits exponentially, allowing the organization to conserve much-needed funds and helping it achieve a higher profile in the community.

The concept of sponsorship isn't new and it isn't limited to charitable causes. Professional sports may be the most extreme example. It's difficult to see the uniforms and cars of NASCAR drivers beneath the multitude of corporate logos that adorn them. Professional football games have multiple sponsors and, in recent years, even the half-time shows and shots of the scoreboards get their own sponsors. Companies pay huge sums to maintain stadium skyboxes to entertain clients, and customarily get to hang large banners with their companies' logos around the stadium. More often than not, stadiums and arenas are now known by the names of the major sponsors that bought naming rights.

In both the private and public sectors, sponsorship means money: The sponsor pays it in hopes of gaining recognition and goodwill and, as a result, more customers. The recipient accepts it to offset the expense of a specific project.

But there's more than one way that companies give money to charities. A few definitions first:

- *Underwriting:* An underwriter is a company or individual that commits to paying all of the event costs or the lion's share. As the primary benefactor, the corporation or person is assured the greatest exposure, ensuring the name will appear on virtually everything connected with the event, including advertisements, invitations, television and radio commercials, news releases, posters, banners at the event and, of course, a prominent position in the program book.

- *Sponsors:* These also can be businesses or individuals that agree to cover the cost of some aspect of the event, such as invitations, food or beverages, the entertainment, awards, or some other portion of the expenses involved in producing the event. Sponsors' names generally feature prominently in the event's promotion material, but would get second billing after a major underwriter.

- *Donation:* This is the simplest form of giving money. A business or a private individual contributes either money or in-kind services—equipment, merchandise, etc.—without expecting a specific amount of publicity (or any at all) in return.

Sponsorship and underwriting come in the forms of money, merchandise, and in-kind services. Sponsors may be local businesses or large corporations, but they may also be individuals who support the cause. Whatever the source, the sponsors' contributions reduce the amount the nonprofit organization must spend to raise money. In return, the charity provides a specific set of benefits to the sponsor that are clearly spelled out in advance.

The process of obtaining sponsors resembles that of most business ventures: When opening a new business, it's customary to line up companies willing to help get things going, to provide initial inventory, and to support the fledgling venture while it gets on its feet. Use that same approach when working on sponsorship for a special event. After creating a realistic budget, but before committing to staging an event, evaluate potential sources of corporate or individual underwriting and sponsorship. Possible sources would include members of the event committee, their personal and business contacts, and prominent local business leaders and their companies. Look for companies or products that regularly appear in full-page ads in national newspapers and magazines, then approach them for sponsorship.

"More and more corporate giving is marketing, not real philanthropy," says David King, a certified fundraising executive who is managing partner and president of Alexander Haas Martin & Partners in Atlanta.

Charities must be able to show companies they approach what they will get for their investment. To that end, the charity should go after sponsorship with marketing information ready. Be prepared to provide specifics on the types of people who will attend, how many are likely to show up, what the group plans to do with the company logo, and how many people will see it.

"That's what corporations are looking for, not that the group serves 250 children a day," King says. Charities "have to think about it the way marketing departments are looking at it. They've got lots of opportunities to sponsor things. Ultimately, they have to make a decision as to how it fits with their own philosophy and how much marketing bang they'll get for it."

When approaching a potential sponsor, have printed information that shows group members have done their homework. It should include the following:

- *Demographics:* The age, income, and gender mix of the group's target market and how that matches the needs of the potential sponsor.
- *Psychographics:* How sponsoring the event or events will give the business exposure to people whose tastes and attitudes would make them likely to embrace the sponsor's product.
- *Market advantage:* If the potential sponsor competes fiercely with other purveyors of a specific product, sponsoring this event might make it more popular with potential customers.
- *Image:* That the event fits the image a sponsor is after and vice versa.
- *Repeated exposure:* A series of events allows a sponsor multiple exposures to its target market. Many sponsors prefer this to a one-time-only arrangement.

For a detailed guide to obtaining the maximum amount of corporate sponsorship, consider investing in the International Events Group's "Guide to Sponsorship," which offers step-by-step directions and advice. It's one of several publications the Chicago-based company offers. For details, check the www.sponsorship.com Web site.

When a charity can demonstrate the benefits to potential sponsors, companies are far more likely to respond positively to the appeal. The promise of advertising in magazines, newspapers, or on television and radio is a strong motivator. Companies that do a lot of sponsorship generally expect a three-for-one return on their investment. That means that if they give $10,000 toward sponsoring the music, they expect $30,000 worth of radio and TV air time in which their company name is mentioned, and space in print advertisements in which their company name and/or logo appear.

But award-winning actor and founder of Newman's Own, Paul Newman maintains that many companies recognize that there is value to corporate sponsorship beyond the dollar figures. As co-founder of the Committee to Encourage Corporate Philanthropy, he has gathered more than 120 CEOs and chairpeople who both advocate and promote corporate philanthropy, not simply because it's good for business.

"All significant stakeholders in a company's success—shareholders, employees and customers—are positively impacted by structured and focused corporate philanthropy initiatives," he wrote in a *Wall Street Journal* Letter to the Editor in April 2006. "An engaged workforce that takes pride in its company creates a corporate culture that improves recruiting and retention, extends brand reputation, strengthens inter-employee relationships and reinforces leadership and teamwork skills. Additional benefits accrue through enhanced consumer, government and media perceptions, which can encourage customer loyalty, grow business development efforts and provide a buffer against potentially negative news, respectively. Furthermore, helping to build a strong and stable social and economic infrastructure considerably strengthens a company's business in the communities in which it operates."

There's no better example of how much some major corporations value philanthropic endeavors than Share Our Strength, a nationwide charitable organization backed by heavy hitters such as American Express and Jenn-Air. The anti-hunger and anti-poverty group holds some 60 Taste of the Nation events around the United States and Canada. There are food and wine tastings, seated dinners, brunches, and barbecues, so that participation isn't limited to the very wealthy. The result: Some 55,000 people attend at least one of the events each year.

The national sponsors team up with local ones to cover virtually all of the costs so that 100 percent of the ticket proceeds go to the charity, which awards grants to organizations that combat hunger and poverty.

Between 1988 and 2005, the events raised about $55 million for the charity and provided invaluable positive publicity to the sponsors and participating chefs and restaurants. Share Our Strength maintains a Web site (www.strength.org) that not only explains what the charity does, but it also includes sections that feature all of the chefs, sponsors, and grant recipients.

It's not possible to place a numerical value on all of the benefits the sponsors receive, but there are some specific facets to which dollar values can be assigned and most companies want to know about them.

> **TIP** *The easier the charity makes it for a company to see how it will benefit from sponsorship, the more likely it is that companies will get involved.*

The Cleveland, Ohio Metropark Zoo makes it easy for potential sponsors to see what their money will buy by spelling it out on its Web site—www.clemetzoo.com. It lists each of the zoo's special events, explains what it is, how many and what type of people typically attend, the sponsorship levels available, what benefits are available, and who to contact, including a phone number and e-mail address.

Twilight at the Zoo, for example, is a party held in August that features 17 bands of varying styles on 15 stages, a VIP area, unlimited food and drink, and other fun that attracts roughly 7,000 affluent, urban professionals ages 25 to 45 years. Sponsorships range from $1,000 to $15,000. Benefits include the sponsor's name and logo included in advertising and promotion, media releases, on-site signage, corporate hospitality, retail tie-ins, complimentary tickets, category exclusivity, and recognition in zoo publications.

By spelling everything out clearly, offering a range of opportunities, and making it easy for sponsors to tie in, the zoo demonstrates its understanding of the varying needs of companies and allows them to target that segment of the zoo's 1.3 million visitors that fits its needs.

The Pin Oak Charity Horse Show in Houston, Texas, employs a similar strategy and, over the course of 60 years, has donated $3 million to worthy causes, primarily those benefiting children. Potential sponsors can go to the show's Web site—www.pinoak.org—and find all they need to know about the show, the charities that benefit, and the sponsorship opportunities available.

Sponsorship opportunities range from $200 to $50,000. At the low end, sponsors receive identification in show publications, one public address announcement per day plus admittance to a dinner and the daily cocktail party, as well as preferred show and parking passes. At the high end, sponsors are guaranteed a full-page color ad in the Pin Oak magazine, a logo on sponsor boards and the Web site, four public address announcements each day, banners, high-traffic-area signs, 18 dinner tickets, 50 preferred show passes, lunch daily, and lots of other perks.

The results are tangible: Among the show's sponsors are Neiman Marcus, Lexus, the *Houston Chronicle*, KTRK-TV (Houston's ABC station), and Dillard's. These big-name companies sign on because they know that some 10,000 people will turn out at the event, giving them great exposure.

One note of caution, however: Many sponsors have become increasingly demanding, often pressuring charities to give them more than before. They might want to be the only sponsor whose logo appears on the stage or they may want exclusivity in their field (a real estate broker, for example, may require that no other real estate agencies be permitted to sponsor if he does). Don't knuckle under to these tactics. If the company wants more than comes with the level of sponsorship it's paying for, make sure it is willing to pay more for that privilege.

Certified fundraising executive David King advises that the charity should send its best negotiator to approach potential sponsors. "Business people are better at negotiating than people in the nonprofit sector," he says. And charity representatives should decide in advance whether they will negotiate with sponsors.

"Corporate executives are accustomed to negotiating everything," King says. "If your lead sponsorship is $10,000, and the budget doesn't work unless you get that, you need to go in with the mindset that this is a non-negotiable thing. Maybe you can negotiate some of the benefits, but not the price."

The International Events Group (www.sponsorship.com), a Chicago-based provider of sponsorship research and analysis, publishes 52 sponsorship contracts, each geared to different types of events and causes in a variety of computer formats so that the charity can tailor the document to its particular situation. The cost is $99 for up to five contracts, then each one costs $15, or get all 52 for $499.

> **TIP** *Check with local chambers of commerce to locate the biggest companies in the region. Many list them on the chamber Web site. Approach those firms first for support.*

Don't forget to look beyond the town or city limits. Conduct a thorough search of the Internet as well, because there are many national firms that have sponsorship programs available to communities in which their products or services are used.

Media First

Before approaching companies for money, try to get a radio station or newspaper—or both—as a sponsor. Generally, the sponsoring media company will provide a certain amount of advertising time/space to promote the event. With the media on board, it's easier to line up sponsorship from other businesses interested in promoting themselves while supporting a worthwhile cause.

When seeking the support of a radio station, pick one whose listeners would be likely to attend the event. All radio station executives know precisely who their listeners are—their ages, median incomes, and listening habits. This is the information they use to sell commercials. Ask to see and examine their demographics. For a chili festival promotion, a country-and-western station would be a likely sponsor because its listeners range widely in age and are generally working-class families most likely to attend the event.

> **TIP** *Radio stations are likely to be more receptive to a charity's request for public service announcements, which are free, if the charity can also offer the station paying commercials from its corporate-sponsor partners.*

If someone in the group has a contact at a newspaper, radio, or television station, request that the member let that person know someone from the group will be calling to seek support for a charitable cause. This can help gain access the charity might not be able to make on its own.

Approach the marketing department first, because that's where the people are who make decisions on sponsorship. Ask if the company has a written procedure for seeking sponsorship. If so, get a copy. It will allow group members to assemble all the information the company will want before a representative makes a pitch. Such proposals are best done in person by a confident representative of the group armed with all necessary information about the event demographics and some background on the event.

Try finding out who in the company makes sponsorship decisions and request to meet with that person. That will save time for everyone concerned and possibly improve the charity's chances of getting support.

(Later, once details of the event are set, then it's time to make contact with the news staff. See Chapter 10, The Media and the Message.)

When seeking support from a national company, the event must draw at least 2,500 people. Make sure the charity can deliver on that promise. If it can't, seek the support of smaller, local firms instead. Among these might be shopping centers, a specific store, or local or regional beverage distributors.

GETTING MAXIMUM SUPPORT

How many sponsors are there with deep pockets? The 2006 sponsorship report by International Events Group (IEG) indicates that the country's most active corporate sponsors are expected to contribute $13.39 billion annually to get their names out through event sponsorship. That's an increase of 10.6 percent over 2005. Of course, there are ever more groups seeking a slice of it. The trick to getting a piece of that very large pie is to know the group's audience and potential sponsors and then clearly illustrate to those sponsors how they will benefit by supporting the organization's efforts.

> **TIP** *Start looking for sponsors and underwriters early—at least six months to a year before the event.*

Among the sources for finding the broadest range of potential sponsors are:

- Look up the names of companies on the Internet or at the library. Major corporate directories, such as Standard & Poor's, provide a lot of information.

- For a large-scale search, the International Events Group (www .sponsorship.com) compiles a sponsorship directory that contains the names of 4,500 top sponsors and what they fund. It comes in book form with a CD-ROM.

- Other offerings available from IEG include indexes to various types of properties; who likes to donate to opera, fine arts, or car racing; how to find the most active sponsors in a particular market; a valuation service that determines fair market value of online and offline sponsorship packages; a guide to Web sponsorship and a sample agreement; and a bi-weekly online newsletter. It also conducts seminars aimed at improving nonprofit organizations' sponsorship savvy.

Although these tools are somewhat pricey, the newsletters alone can pay for themselves and can save the organization hours and hours of work—work that someone else has already done and updates yearly.

OTHER CREATIVE SPONSORSHIPS

Whole Foods Market, a national chain of supermarkets, offers a 5 percent day once a month, during which 5 percent of all sales go to a specific charity. Each store has a team of people that decides which charities benefit. The causes change each month, giving a variety of causes a chance to get a share of the proceeds.

PETsMART provides extensive support to animal-related charities. Its PETsMART Charities supports programs to help sterilize animals, offers disaster assistance, and will even dispense grants for nonprofit animal welfare groups to buy much-needed equipment. In the decade since it was founded in 1994, the charity donated $39 million to more than 3,400 animal-welfare groups. (It also offers annual Web-based conferences on e-philanthropy and other fundraising topics.)

Many other large companies offer similar types of sponsorship. It is worth checking around to see if there are any the organization could get involved in. If not, consider approaching a regional store to begin such a program, which would give it good community visibility.

TAPPING INTO MONEY

One way to drum up local support is with an underwriting party. Draw up a list of the things for which the group would like to secure financial backing. Check the budget sheet to make sure everything is included.

Prior to the party, distribute the list of items and what each costs—these can be sent along with a letter of invitation that asks the recipients if they'd like to help underwrite the event by making a cash donation. Then invite everyone to the underwriting party, at which it's customary to serve cocktails and light fare. By drawing potential sponsors to the pre-event, they get involved and might feel motivated to do more for the coming event.

At the party, spend five to ten minutes either discussing the missions and accomplishments of the group or, better yet, show a short video that includes testimonials from people the charity has helped or bring in some of the people themselves to speak. Next, announce the sponsorship commitments already received and thank those companies for their participation. Then it's time to hand out the list of things that remain to be underwritten, what the benefits are at each level of sponsorship, and encourage those who haven't yet done so to pitch in.

Some groups assign sponsorship chores to the event coordinator or someone that person designates. Others use a committee to contact potential sponsors for support. Usually, the more influential businesspeople on the committee, the broader their reach and the more underwriting they will get.

> **TIP** *Networking is a great way to get a sponsorship program started. Bring together a committee that includes many influential, well-connected people who know the people in a position to provide significant underwriting. Virtually every town has chapters of Kiwanis or Rotary as well as chambers of commerce, all of which meet regularly and include a cross-section of the business community.*

FOLLOWING UP

After a company ponies up and the event takes place, some of the charity's most important work is yet to be done. First, write each sponsor a thank-you note. This should not be a form letter. Include the following information:

- How many people attended.
- Copies of everything that appeared in print in which the sponsor's name was mentioned—flyers, invitations, advertisements, tickets, program books.
- Photos of whatever promotional material was displayed at the event, such as banners, a display, or a booth (try to photograph these when there are a lot of people around them).

- An advertising schedule that shows how often public service announcements or advertisements of the event were broadcast.
- Assign values to each of the preceding items and itemize it so the sponsor can see the dollar value of participation.

Finally, if the group can afford it, purchase a display ad in the local newspaper to thank all of the sponsors. It's an added expense but goes a long way toward making those who are recognized feel appreciated and favorably inclined to support the cause again.

Some newspapers print information about charitable events. In order to have the best chance of getting such exposure, make sure the photos and news release arrive the day after the event. Contact the newspaper in advance and ask news staff to cover the event, but the charity should plan to have its own photographer and someone to write a few cogent, concise paragraphs. With the advent of digital photography and e-mail, this is easy to accomplish.

Several weeks after the event, contact sponsors once more and ask if they would like to sign on for the following year. Chances are, if they were happy with how things went, they will agree. Ask them to consider a larger sponsorship.

CONFLICTS OF INTEREST

Sometimes there are conflicts between a charity's mission and those of the corporations that want to underwrite an event. Some conflicts are obvious, such as a tobacco company sponsoring a lung association or cancer society event. Charities must be vigilant in checking for situations with the potential for such problems. Although the corporation's intentions may be sincere, if potential donors find the connection offensive, the company's participation may hinder, rather than enhance, fundraising.

Even if a particular sponsor doesn't fit with the event being planned now, if the problem is handled with sensitivity, chances are that would-be sponsor will be willing to provide support to a more appropriate future event.

On Location

Real estate isn't the only business in which location looms large. Where an event takes place can be as critical to its success as the group's mission and the nature of the event itself. The locale has to be attractive, yet functional. Accessible, but intriguing. Affordable without appearing cheap. It must also possess ample parking in a safe neighborhood.

Everyone has attended events in what seem like fairy-tale settings—a perfectly restored historic home filled with period antiques; or a grand, marble-laden ballroom with sparkling crystal chandeliers; or a lavishly decorated circus tent. While they are all lovely locales, the odds are that every one of those events was privately funded by someone for whom money was not a primary concern.

Usefulness, not beauty, is most often the best measurement of a site's suitability when it comes to charitable events. The exception to this is if an underwriter pays for the spectacular site and it's clear to everyone who attends that the charity did not spend extravagantly.

RESEARCHING THE RIGHT SITE

When brainstorming about sites, expect committee members to suggest places based on their experiences. In most cases, those experiences began after the site was spruced up. People generally have no clue how much time and money it takes to make a place beautiful and functional.

It is up to the event coordinator and chairperson to thoroughly research sites under consideration to make sure the final choice is a practical one,

95

rather than giving in to committee members' enthusiasm for a site that's beautiful, but that would require an exorbitant amount of money to make usable. Do not seek the biggest, flashiest, most expensive venue in town. Instead, find one that can provide the basics at a price that fits the group's budget and leaves sufficient funds for decorating. Of course, the best of all possibilities is to find a site that meets all the practical needs of the event and also has aesthetic appeal.

> **TIP** *Enlist the advice of party designers to estimate costs of producing events at the venues under consideration.*

It may seem like a monumental task to find that ideal spot, but a systematic approach helps simplify the process.

SITE CONSIDERATIONS

There are four primary factors to consider when assessing a site:

1. Location
2. Cost
3. Size
4. Facilities

It's up to the event coordinator and chair people to assess how these apply to the event under consideration.

Location

First, develop a list of potential sites. Look for articles on social events held at imaginative sites in magazines such as *People, In Style, Town & Country*, as well as upscale local magazines and newspapers and, of course, the Internet.

Check out the Yellow Pages, and conduct an Internet search for local churches, halls, caterers, hotels, restaurants, parks, historic sites, and recreation areas. With some creativity, a farm field, park, or gigantic parking lot can hold top-notch events. In colder climates, other possibilities include ice skating rinks and ski resorts. In warmer locales, consider public beaches. Establish a file of sites for future reference.

Do not dismiss a site simply because it appears plain at first. There are occasions when minimalism is both desirable and lucrative.

Take the humble field, for example, the perfect spot for cow-chip bingo, which requires only the aforementioned field and a well-fed bovine. Just mark off squares on the field, sell each one for a set amount ($25 or so), then place the cow on it and let the chips fall where they may. The person who possesses the piece of field that the cow graces by depositing her chips is the winner. This event needs little setup or upfront financial outlay, requires few committee members, and can quickly and easily raise upwards of $75,000. Sell food and raffle tickets and that figure quickly climbs.

A few lesser-known, but often quite serviceable locations include airplane hangars, public gardens, lighthouses, museums, plantations, parks, stadiums, boats, shopping centers, country clubs, schools, and wineries.

Consider renting out a whole restaurant—or a bare banquet room—and create a theme or look if the group cannot find a ready-made site that's suitable. Unusual sites will vary from city to city, but what works elsewhere might well lend itself to adaptation.

A different strategy is to use the location as a draw in itself. That's what Great Performances does with the Frederick P. Rose Hall, home of the nonprofit Jazz at Lincoln Center. Since it opened in the fall of 2004, the structure has become a major attraction for charitable causes. The vast building stands over Manhattan's Columbus Circle, providing sweeping views of Central Park and Manhattan's impressive skyline, particularly from the atrium with its floor-to-ceiling windows. There are also two performing art arenas, a recording studio, a media room, and two multi-purpose rooms so that the building is both visually appealing and well-suited to a variety of activities for large and small groups.

"People come because of the space," says Linda Abbey, vice president of Great Performances, which holds an exclusive catering contract with the venue. "They haven't seen it and are interested. They may feel a loyalty to the charity and the location is that extra little hook you can provide to reel them in."

Another option is to offer a place where most people ordinarily aren't admitted. Special-location gatherings can raise substantial sums if they are held in a spectacular home, a unique corporate setting, or other unusual location, and chaired by high-powered, but usually inaccessible, executives.

The Naples Winter Wine Fest, the highest-grossing charity wine auction in the country, raises millions for children's charities, in part because of the combination of locations it employs. Firstly, it's held in late January in tony, subtropical Naples, Florida. On Friday morning, guests get a chance to meet beneficiaries of the millions raised in previous auctions by the Naples Children & Education Foundation, the charity that sponsors the festival. That evening, they attend dinner at one of 18 private estates owned by the charity's trustees. Each dinner features a celebrity chef and vintner pairing up food and wine. Past guest chefs include Emeril Lagasse, Thomas Keller, Charlie Trotter, and Todd English. On Saturday, the party continues at The Ritz-Carlton Golf Resort, where the auction of wine, travel packages, and other high-end fare takes place under a tent. The weekend concludes with a Sunday brunch at The Ritz. The 2006 festival raised close to $14 million for the charities it supports.

Few charities have the deep pockets and clout it requires to stage such a multifaceted event or access to the sumptuous homes and hotels available in Naples, but the event's success illustrates what's possible.

For most charitable groups, creativity and imagination applied to more modest settings are the ingredients that will produce a profitable event.

Develop a list of possible locations, then fill out a location survey form for each. Check Web sites for each establishment to get as much information as possible, then phone each to fill in gaps and make sure the Web information is current. Compare the surveys and eliminate sites that are too small, too large, too expensive, or too booked up.

After narrowing down the choices to two or three, ask each site's manager for the names and telephone numbers of contact people from other organizations that have held events there. Call someone from each group to find out how the events turned out, how well the site met their needs, and what shortcomings or strengths they discovered.

Another possibility is a location that allows group members to forget about budgets, menus, and other bothersome details. Companies such as Voyages Unlimited (vacations.voyagesunlimited.com) and Carnival Cruise Lines offer fundraising opportunities to charities whose members are cruise enthusiasts. This makes for a fun and effective fundraiser for organizations with ten or more chapters and a mailing list of 3,500 or more contributors who give $500 or more annually to charity.

The companies provide cruises at a group rate and the charity can designate an amount above that which will go to the charitable cause. In most cases, the company and the cruise line will match all or a portion of the amount the charity gets.

While the group is cruising, the charity can also stage an auction, golf tournament, on-board walk-a-thon, black-tie dinner, special receptions with celebrities, and seminars designed to raise money and develop allegiances to the cause.

The Location of Locations

In most cases, people drive to the event. When considering a site, think about how easy it is to find. If it is an evening event, will people feel safe driving there at night? Is there adequate parking close to the building?

Sometimes the location is fixed and the event organizers must work around it. Such was the case when the new Kenneth Cole shoe store opened in the high-fashion district of Miami Beach's chic South Beach. The three-story store held a maximum of 150 people, but 700 to 900 guests were expected. In order to accommodate the large group, the event coordinator obtained a permit to close the street in front of the store and tented half of it. People could walk in and out of the tent, wander into the store, sample hors d'oeuvres, and mingle with celebrities such as Cole, Calvin Klein, and Diddy (formerly P. Diddy).

During the opening party and throughout the following week, the store donated 10 percent of its sales to support Health Crisis Network, an AIDS service organization in Miami. The invitation read: "You might have to pull some strings to get into this party." Inside was a shoelace. Kenneth Cole Shoes paid for the entire event, so all the money raised went to the Health Crisis Network.

Cost

What can the group afford? (Refer to the budget worksheet in Chapter 2, Money Matters.)

The real trick is balancing affordability and aesthetic appeal. "You can spend an extraordinary amount of money making a cheap place look fabulous," says Shelley Clark, vice president of Lou Hammond & Associates, a New York-based public relations firm. "You have to weigh that carefully" when choosing a site.

A well-equipped restaurant or hotel may prove less expensive in the long run because everything needed to produce an event is already there. With a bare-bones site, renting and trucking in tables and chairs, dishes, linens, flowers, decorations, and all the other necessary niceties can quickly add up.

Conversely, in states in which hotel and restaurant employees are unionized, such as New York, these venues are likely to be more costly because labor expenses are higher, Clark says.

Whatever the venue, remember to inquire how much setup time is permitted. It can take several hours to prepare a room for an event what with arranging tables, chairs, dishes, décor, and staging. Make sure the group has access to the room in time and what (if any) additional costs might be involved.

For some events, such as fashion shows, it may take a full day to set up. In these cases, it may be necessary to reserve the room for the whole day. The establishment may charge extra for tying up the room that long, although some raise the price of the food instead.

> **TIP** *Find out who will be using the room before the event and what decorations they will be using. If their décor fits with the group's plan, ask the previous occupant to leave the decorations and donate them to the group. That saves the charity the expense of buying and setting up more decorations, and the previous group saves time cleaning up.*

Size

Never mind conventional wisdom. When it comes to holding an event, size matters. "It's always tricky," says Linda Abbey, of Great Performances, a New York-based caterer and production company. "You know based on previous history how many people came, so you don't want to book something so small that you can't fit in more. You want as many people to come and pay as possible. You have to make an educated guess."

The type of event factors into this, too. Less space is necessary to hold 200 people for a cocktail party than for a sit-down dinner for the same number. If the crowd just barely fit into the room last year and the group plans to add a fashion or stage show this time, find a larger space. When it comes to fashion shows, runways can play havoc with space.

Many venues now list the capacity of their various rooms on their Web sites. However, it never hurts for organizers to make their own calculations.

TIP *How much room is enough? Here are some basic guidelines:*

- *For stand-up buffets and receptions, figure on 8 to 10 square feet per person.*
- *For a show in a theater or auditorium, plan on 10 to 12 square feet per person.*
- *For a seated banquet, count on about 12 square feet per person.*
- *Add 2 square feet per person if there will be dancing as well.*
- *For meals at tented events, don't forget to calculate space for the kitchen and prep tents.*

Make a list of activities, then mentally walk through the event:

- *Where will the registration table go?*
- *Where will people have cocktails?*
- *Where are they going to eat dinner?*
- *Where will the stage be?*
- *Where will the actors dress?*
- *Will there be a reception line? If so, where will it form?*

Take precise measurements of the site. Multiply the length by the width to get the total square footage. Subtract space for areas that block views or impede traffic.

Site Facilities

Picking a site can be like buying a dress or suit: At first glance, it may look good despite a less-than–perfect fit. But the first time it's worn in public, all its flaws become obvious. A site that looks good but doesn't have the facilities to accommodate the group's event can set the stage for a disaster. While everyone wants an attractive site, remember that the decorations committee can do much to beautify a less-than-perfect site. What's needed are basics, such as adequate parking, enough space for the number of people expected to attend, sufficient kitchen and bathroom facilities, and staff.

An event held at an outdoor site can cost thousands of dollars to bring in things such as portable toilets, electricity, lights, sound equipment, flooring, air conditioning or heating, and maybe a tent. Even then, that won't guarantee that Mother Nature will look kindly upon the proceedings. Such considerations are why more than two-thirds of all events take place in hotels, halls, auditoriums, theaters, or houses of worship.

Think about other items an event might require. Besides the primary site at which the event occurs, most need still more space for a registration area, a place to prepare food and one to serve it from, and perhaps a spot for a piano or musical trio to perform during cocktails. And then there are the general convenience factors: Where will the event be in relation to a coatroom, rest rooms, and parking.

Besides being an appropriate size, a site plays a part in shaping the décor. Barton G. Weiss, who heads up the multifaceted Barton G. event planning, production, and catering company, believes that the look of the event should blend with the food being served to engage the senses, rather than aiming for the most opulent look.

"I'm trying to get away from themes like casino night or midsummer night's dream," he says. "Instead, I'm trying to come up with a feel rather than a theme." He favors well-designed spaces with interesting structure. Rather than plaster the room with themed items, he prefers to downplay the glitz and use a mix of fabrics and textures to provide a sensual feel.

"The challenge is that every charity wants a signature," Weiss says. "Every charity wants to be the most memorable event of the season. How do you keep doing that?" In the winter of 2007, he's staging a gala for a large hospital that will be a winter fest featuring a monochromatic, white-on-white look. He's also done a Cat in the Hat ball.

"It was a huge hit," he says. "One table had a cockeyed fishbowl, another had a cockeyed cake. We all grew up with it. It's clever, innovative and fresh. Adults trying to be kids, that's the fun of it. They were all walking around by the end of the night with Cat in the Hat hats on."

SETTING SITES

After phoning the sites and checking their references, it should be easy to come up with three top choices. Either the event coordinator or chair or both should inspect the sites, particularly the kitchens, ballrooms, and parking. They should talk with the banquet manager to see if it's a good fit for their group. They should ask the manager if the staff regularly works at the site or is hired on an as-needed basis from an agency. Results are generally better when the staff is consistent and familiar with the site.

Once the group has picked a site, get a copy of the site plan in order to map out how to use the space. Most ballrooms have table plans that have been used successfully at previous buffets, fashion shows, and such. Ask for seating plans if they aren't forthcoming.

Also inquire as to whether the venue would allow a group member or two to observe a similar event scheduled in the near future. Groups not working with a hotel and without a selection of room setups can devise their own plans using any of a number of software packages that make this a relatively simple process.

> TIP *For parking, figure on about half as many spaces as people you expect. There should be one valet per twenty-five cars.*

First, create a site plan. Map entrances and exits, the light switches, the sound system controls, the bathrooms, the coatroom, first-aid area, trash dumpster, and parking. Consider what events will take place and how traffic should flow. When possible, arrange to observe a similar event at the site as the one the group is planning.

Doing a walk-through of the event in the empty room can help determine what goes where. Sometimes the location just won't accommodate everything in one place. If there isn't one room big enough for everything, figure out a way to use several areas of the site, perhaps arranging several small dining areas, with food set up in another spot, entertainment another. Once the group settles on how to use the space, make sure it is all spelled out in the contract—before signing anything, paying a deposit, and sending out the invitations.

CHAPTER 7

Food, Glorious and Otherwise

The old axiom about food being the way to a lover's heart holds equally true for charities wooing would-be donors. Food can make an event—or break it, if costs spiral out of control. It can also affect a charity's reputation if the event proves memorable because the food was terrible.

Considering how many events take place these days and that most involve food in some form, keeping it fresh, interesting, and appetizing gets ever tougher.

"My job has gotten harder over the years," says events impresario Barton G. Weiss, the Miami-based founder and head of Barton G., a business empire that includes a restaurant, a catering service, and an events production company. "People are getting jaded. I've spent the past two years fusing food and décor," striving to make the experience more stimulating to all of the senses.

"Food is becoming the entertainment rather than bringing in a celebrity," Weiss says. "We're making it interactive, whimsical. People love to go back to childhood. It's all about entertainment and creating the memory. I like to do the unexpected, like for dessert serving cotton candy or a big ice cream sundae."

Linda Abbey, vice president of Great Performances, a New York-based catering and events management company, uses some similar strategies. She's served warm chocolate chip cookies with milk shooters and shot glasses filled with jelly beans to add elements of delight to her events. "These people see everything," she says, so surprising them takes imagination.

In Fort Myers, Florida, the Lee County AIDS Task Force held a highly unusual food event that raised $15,000 for the cause. It held a chocolate-and-cheese dinner at Cru, one of the city's hippest restaurants. Patrons paid $250 per ticket to attend the seven-course meal conjured up by renowned pastry chef and chocolatier Norman Love and cheese maven Caroline Hostettler. The two teamed up to create course after course that combined the two elements in intriguing ways. Fare included a chocolate martini with a gorgonzola olive and fried chocolate focaccia with stacchino cream, fig compote, and port reduction.

The restaurant donated the space and staff, Love and Hostettler donated their time and talents so all of the money from the tickets when to the charity. Love, Hostettler, and Cru reaped lots of media coverage and customer loyalty from a crowd that loved the fanciful dishes, all of which looked like works of art.

CRITICAL DETAILS

Besides the quality of what is served, groups need to pay attention to time limitations .Weiss operates on the premise that a party has a specified life span: "You've got $3\frac{1}{2}$ hours to do your thing, I don't care how amazing (the event) is," he says. To make the most of that time, he recommends scaling back the 90-minute cocktail period, during which people cluster in small groups and don't mingle. Instead, head straight to the main attraction and crank up the energy level early. "The fun of it is the party," he says.

In keeping with his philosophy of doing the unexpected and melding the food with the action, he had all 450 guests at one gala change tables for each course of a sit-down meal.

Besides serving as a primary attraction, food generally represents the biggest expense, too, unless there's a big-name entertainer, so it is critical to calculate into the budget both best- and worst-case scenarios for food and related expenses.

No matter how spectacular an event looks, if the food or service is poor, that's what people will remember and talk about. "People love to eat and I think even the least sophisticated consumer is more sophisticated now than 10 years ago," says Linda Abbey. That means the food must both look and taste good. That's just one reason a tasting well in advance of the event is a must.

"I want the client happy," she says. "I'm describing one thing and you may be envisioning another. What's spicy to one is not hot enough to someone else. A tasting is a win-win for everybody."

Abbey says there's nothing wrong with serving chicken or salmon, rather than beef, lamb, duck, or more expensive varieties of seafood.

"We have been serving a lot of fish," she says, recalling a recent event for 400 at Sotheby's at which her company served miso-glazed sea bass. "We watched the plates come back," Abbey says. "It was devoured."

During the spring and summer, when people want lighter fare, seafood makes an excellent entrée, she says. Nonetheless, steak may still win out. "Everybody loves a great cut of beef," Abbey says, although she finds that people are more open to change these days than in the past.

While preparing steak to the divergent tastes assembled at a dinner may be standard operating procedure for big, polished operations such as Great Performances and Barton G., culinary capability varies with every venue. Remember that steak can be difficult to serve to a large number of guests at once so carefully assess the skill level of the kitchen when making menu decisions.

Not every event will include a sit-down meal. Instead of the big dinner-dance, many organizations now choose less labor-intensive and less costly ways to raise money and, in the process, significantly scale back food and beverage costs.

Instead of an involved multi-course meal, consider holding a welcoming reception prior to a show or lecture, provided that all the guests have purchased tickets from the charity and the charity has use of the entire facility. Those who attend receive one free glass of wine or champagne and can purchase additional drinks if they wish. This can cost the charity little or no money if a liquor distributor donates the beverages, or someone underwrites the expense.

If the group has a higher-priced ticket level for patrons and benefactors, refreshments might get a bit more elaborate at a private "Patrons Only" reception following the performance, with the celebrity in attendance. This sort of event takes place at about 9:30 p.m., so it's perfectly acceptable to pass hot and cold hors d'oeuvres or offer pasta at serving stations or a lavish dessert buffet, with champagne and fancy coffees and teas.

Both Weiss and Abbey believe a sit-down meal works more effectively than buffets in most cases. "I've not seen a lot of non–sit-down fund-raisers by major charities," Abbey says. "Most causes want to get people in a seat."

An event for young up-and-comers who may not be able to afford an expensive dinner might be an exception to that rule. In such a case, a cocktail party with hors d'oeuvres would be fine and need not be a sit-down affair.

But for most events, Weiss believes the sit-down style fits better. "At a seated dinner, there's more drama, its theater," he says. "You can create that whole anticipation, the whole feel of the wow. I tend never to do buffets unless it's casual and it's only for a two-hour period."

He also advises not to break into the middle of the meal with speeches, lengthy programs, or videos. If the group plans to deliver a message about its mission, he thinks it's best done early, before the dinner, drinking, and socializing rev into high gear.

"There are only so many peaks and valleys you can have in an evening," Weiss says. "Two times and you're done. You don't get three strikes here. Once you build up the energy and anticipation (perhaps with dance music and a DJ) you've got to let the party go. You can't stop it with speeches, you can't stop it with big programs and videos. Don't oversaturate the evening trying to legitimize why people are there. People know why they're there."

Again, there may be exceptions to the rule here, too. Sometimes timing dictates that the meal and the program happen simultaneously.

For events at which there's a time constraint—a longer-than-average program or a shorter span for the event—there are ways to speed up even a traditional sit-down meal, says Abbey.

"Do two courses instead of three," she says, then offer a dessert and coffee buffet, as her firm did at a recent event. "People could go there or go home. For the most part, people stayed."

Still, there are occasions when an event must include elaborate food and drink. Here are some ways to lessen the likelihood of gastronomic disaster or financial ruin as a result.

There are five primary factors that play large roles in determining what type of food to serve:

1. **Demographics:** Determine who will likely attend and what they are apt to eat.

   Many people are more health-conscious than in the past, but may relax those standards when attending an expensive event. Always offer a low-calorie option, but expect most people to select heartier fare. If children attend, make sure there are kid-friendly options such as pizza, hot dogs, and hamburgers.

Religious beliefs and dietary restrictions are important considerations, too. That means no pork for the Hadassah group, no foie gras for the animal rights gathering, and no chocolate volcano cakes for heart-attack recovery groups. During Lent, have fish available and during Passover offer items that contain no bread or yeast. Many other groups have specific restrictions as well so it pays to ask well ahead of the scheduled event.

2. **Scope:** Will there be 50 people or 500 coming? The smaller the group, the less complicated the planning for a meal, because it will require fewer servers, less equipment, dishes, and rental items.

3. **Location:** Will the meal be served indoors or outdoors? Assess the kitchen facilities and determine what is possible to prepare there.

4. **Time:** Consider what's appropriate to serve for the time of day of the event. Breakfasts are usually the lightest meals of the day, lunches a bit more substantial, dinners the most elaborate. A buffet can be tailored to whatever time of day it takes place. Factor in the time of year, too. Foods should suit the season. Out-of-season menus can be extremely costly, and in some cases, inappropriate (such as heirloom tomato gazpacho on a sub-zero night).

5. **Money:** How much can the group spend? Is the event's main purpose making friends or raising money? If the goal is to make a profit, carefully consider the food budget. Unless it is a high-priced event or there is sufficient underwriting, choose a moderately priced but interesting meal.

Think back to events at which the food was memorable for all the right reasons. Seek input from friends and colleagues about their experiences, good and bad, with food served at events. Then consult the executive directors of events at which the food was noteworthy. Inquire who and what they chose, and why. Before signing anything, try out the food in each of the venues under consideration. Some hotels let potential customers observe other events to get an idea of how the staff handles them.

When planning a meal, consider other activities that will take place. If there's a ceremony or awards show planned following dinner, the meal needs to be concluded quickly in order to proceed to the program. Ask the catering manager for an estimate of how long it will take to serve the meal under consideration.

If it's an elaborate, multi-course affair, speed things along by having the first course already set on the tables, so guests can begin eating as soon as they enter the room. Or start the program during the first course, getting some of the speeches out of the way without interference from clattering dishes.

Conversely, at an auction (see Chapter 8, Auctions and Other Profit Boosters), bars should remain open throughout the bidding so people aren't tempted to go home once they've eaten.

IDEAS FOR MEALS, FOOD, AND SETTINGS

Here are some ideas to consider:

Breakfast
- Coffee lovers—cappuccino, espresso, specialty coffees, pastries, fruit
- Country style—eggs, sausage, grits, biscuits and gravy
- Pancake—pancakes, sausages or bacon, fruit
- Jewish—lox (nova, please), bagels, cream cheese

Brunch (Generally Buffet)
- Two choices each of seasonal fruits, rolls and pastries, two vegetables or salad, plus rounds of beef or turkey
- A "stations" setup, such as a pasta station, omelet station, waffle station, and a carving station at which a server cuts beef, turkey, or pork to order

Light Lunch
- Salad with rolls, fruit

Gourmet Lunch
- Soup (chilled in warm weather), well-presented chicken or seafood dish, pasta or fruit salad, rich dessert

Buffet Lunch
- Usually ten to twelve dishes, including meats, salads, fruit, cheeses, breads, and desserts

Casual Dinner
- Cookout with burgers and hot dogs, ribs or chicken
- Pig roast
- Fish fry
- Pasta
- Chili and cornbread
- Pizza
- Potluck or covered dish. Divide guests into three groups by last name. One group brings main courses, the next side dishes, the last desserts. Everyone should bring enough for four to six servings; the sponsoring organization usually provides plates, silverware, and beverages.

Dinner Buffet
- Generally twenty or more choices, including meats, salads, vegetables, fruit, cheese, breads, and desserts
- Heavy hors d'oeuvres

Theme Dinners
- Chinese, Japanese, Italian, French, Cuban, Californian, Hawaiian, Mexican, seafood, vegetarian, etc.

Miscellaneous
- Afternoon tea with finger sandwiches, pastries, coffee, tea
- Sundae bar (guests make their own)

Festival Food
- Chili cookoff
- Pie bakeoff
- Festival: Seafood, watermelon, chocolate, peach, tomato, apple, pumpkin, cherry, strawberry, garlic, spicy foods, Indian, Greek, vegetarian, etc.

Taste of the Town
- A collection of restaurants offer small samples of their appetizers, entrees, and desserts.

This is just a sample of the types of food options possible. The food committee members are likely to have the best sense of what would appeal most to the target audience.

Banquets generally consist of three to five courses. Pick a main course and structure the rest of the meal around it. Whatever the choice, make sure to provide alternatives for those who do not eat meat or are on special diets. Try to achieve a balance of food groups when planning the menu.

Having an interesting meal does not have to cost a fortune. Here is a sample luncheon menu that is both creative and moderately priced:

Luncheon for ± \$30 per person
- Florida citrus salad with assorted field greens and raspberry vinaigrette
- Chicken Wellington with sauce
- Julienne of fresh vegetables
- White and wild rice
- Laced doily with chocolate base filled with lemon, mango, and raspberry sorbets, fresh berries, and coulis
- Coffee and tea

Buffets

These are the easiest types of meals to serve when faced with a small kitchen; a large crowd; a shortage of tables, chairs, or servers; or other circumstances in which a sit-down dinner would be difficult to pull off.

Sometimes a buffet takes longer than a sit-down meal if the stations aren't large enough and it takes people a long time to get their food. This can make it harder to keep to a strict, predetermined schedule. Buffets also may not be appropriate for a formal affair. Many people dislike carrying food (especially anything with a dark sauce) across a room when they are formally dressed. In such cases, consider a modified buffet in which the first course (soup or salad) is on the table when the guests are seated, the main course is served at the table, then dessert and coffee are offered buffet style.

> **TIP** *Don't assume a buffet will be less expensive, especially for a small group. Buffets are often charged on a one-and-a-half portion-per-person basis rather than the single portion-per-person charged for a served, sit-down dinner.*

Moveable Feasts

Dine-arounds, or progressive dinners, have enjoyed popularity in recent years. Guests move from location to location for each course. Progressive dinners can be hosted in several restaurants, hotels, private homes, or a mix of the three.

Light Refreshments

Not every event requires a full-scale meal. If the budget is tight, or the event takes place at a time when no meal is called for, consider serving a variety of snacks, a wine- or alcohol-enhanced punch, and soft drinks with finger foods.

Hotel Food

The greatest advantage to holding an event in a hotel is that it provides everything (food, room, setup, staging, personnel), whereas rented halls and other sites generally do not.

If the group plans to work with a hotel, first set an appointment with the catering director or banquet manager. These people have years of experience in planning events for groups of all sizes.

Clearly communicate the charity's needs by providing the answers to the following questions: Will guests be young or old? Do they have any religious, health, or other food restrictions? Are they accustomed to eating early or late? What else is planned during the event? How long will it take to serve the courses selected?

Be prepared with the facts and figures and a reasonable estimate of the group's budget. Give the catering director or banquet manager a fact sheet about the organization with some specifics about what the group hopes to accomplish and the event's fundraising goal.

Ask that the chef attend the meeting to discuss menus with a group representative and the catering director or banquet manager. In most cases, the catering director will provide a choice of menus suitable for the type of people and event. This includes an estimate of food costs and allows group members to negotiate changes in recipes to fit the budget. Ask for details on how the food will be presented, portion sizes, how long the meal takes to serve, and the number of service staff available. Be sure staff costs are included.

> **TIP** *Ask that the hotel not serve an identical meal at other events several weeks prior to the event.*

At the initial meeting, finalize the date and which room(s) will be used for the reception and dinner. Ask to visit the hotel to taste the food prior to making a commitment. Negotiate with the reservations desk on how many hotel rooms the group will need for overnight guests. If pressed, most hotels will provide a free conference room or several free small hotel rooms for use by the main volunteers who have worked most of that day so they can stay and change into their event clothes.

Before signing a contract, check with other organizations about their experiences with the hotels under consideration. Insist on an itemized bid. Make sure everything has been included and that there are no hidden extras. Always ask if the figure includes parking and the extra rooms needed and make sure that it's clearly spelled out in writing.

Ask the banquet manager how the serving staff is usually dressed. If the group wants something different, expect to pay dearly for it. Most hotels have a standard set of table linens, dishes, glassware, and silverware. Anything more exotic will cost extra. In most cases, so will candles, fancy candlesticks, and anything else not customarily provided. Try to negotiate these small extras and have them included at no cost on the hotel's event estimate.

The decorating committee or party planner can provide these, but it is more convenient and less costly to get these items or other small special services free from a hotel that would like to satisfy the organization so it will patronize the hotel again.

> **TIP** *Hotels quote meal costs separately from tax and gratuities (which can add 18 to 25 percent). Other items generally not included are hors d'oeuvres and beverages.*

Because using a banquet room is included in the price of meals, hotels are usually particular about which group gets which room. Consequently, the larger the group and the more costly the meal, the bigger the ballroom it will get. Don't inflate the number of people anticipated just to get the big room. An event attended by 250 people will look like a failure in a room that holds 500.

> **TIP** *When using rental items, designate a spotter to check items as they are unpacked to ensure everything is there, and do the same thing at the end of the event, making sure everything is returned undamaged to the rental company.*

Hotels usually require a guarantee of the number of guests expected to attend a week before the event. The hotel uses this number to determine how much food to buy, how many people will be needed to prepare and serve, and how much setup time is needed. The final guarantee must be given 24 to 48 hours before the event.

Provide that guarantee in writing because this number determines how many people the charity pays for. The hotel will charge for at least that many guests and will add on for any extras that show up. However, if the group guarantees 250 people and only 200 show, the group still pays for 250.

Hotels customarily prepare for 10 to 15 percent more than the guarantee, so factor that in when giving a figure. (They are also prepared with substitute meals for vegetarians and others with dietary restrictions.)

Most hotels require a 50 percent deposit for a group's first event there. Organizations that have ongoing events at a particular hotel may only have to put down 10 to 20 percent. Deposits are usually nonrefundable. Final payment is customarily due the night of the event, based on the guarantee; additional billing follows. The group needs to make sure it has enough money to pay in advance for these things.

Many hotels require the organization to provide liability insurance or pay for coverage under their umbrella policy.

CATERERS

Outside of a hotel, all of these services are available by hiring a full-service caterer. Besides preparing the food, a full-service caterer sets up and cleans up, provides rentals and staff, and often decorations or staging.

Partial-service caterers are generally less expensive than full-service. Group members might have to rent tables and chairs, tents, and cooking equipment, hire staff, and buy decorations. Remember to add in the costs of these when preparing the budget.

The least expensive option is a no-service caterer who simply prepares the food and drops it off. Who serves it, how, and on what is up to the event organizers.

As with hotels, ask the caterer to provide samples of the menu under consideration. Caterers also require a guarantee for the number of people attending. They usually require a firm guarantee at least a week in advance, because they need to purchase food and coordinate the rental of equipment. They generally build a 10 percent cushion into the guarantee for food and rentals.

In addition to charging for food on a per-person basis, a full-service caterer charges for serving staff on an hourly basis, usually with a three-hour minimum. The number of staff is based on the number of guests attending.

Here's a basic guideline for the ratio of staff to guests:

- For a sit-down meal, one server per 20 guests.
- For a buffet, one server per 40 guests.
- For sit-down or buffet, one captain per 250 guests.
- For a cocktail party, one or two bartenders per 100 guests, and one or two waiters per 100 guests (depending on how extensive the menu is).

The exception to these numbers is when the servers are unionized, with rules that require a specific number of workers. These numbers are not negotiable no matter how worthwhile the charity's cause.

Caterers also charge for equipment rental (and a percentage markup for acquiring it for the client). Always ask what the markup will be, and ask to see the actual rental bill to ensure there are no overcharges.

> **TIP** *Check the contract to make sure there are no duplicate bills, or charges for rental of equipment that is already on site.*

Get an itemized estimate from the caterer that separates the food costs per person from all additional rentals and staff charges. There may be an additional charge for cleanup crews.

Like a hotel, caterers require a deposit (which is separate from the deposit required to reserve the site), and have guidelines for refunds in the event of cancellation. Know exactly what the cancellation policy is. Be sure that the caterer and the event site have coordinated setup times, cleanup responsibilities, equipment usage policies, security, and parking. As with hotels, the organization may be required to provide liability insurance.

> **TIP** *Check with the local health department—or whatever agency inspects commercial kitchens—to see if the caterer has been cited for any health violations.*

ALL DRESSED UP

Ask the caterer what the staff will wear—usually, dark pants, white shirt, and dark tie. As at hotels, if the group wants something different to match the theme, there will be extra charges for uniform rentals. Generally, it isn't necessary to have special outfits, but there are occasions when it makes a difference.

For example, the White Party, which marked its twenty-first year in 2005, is among the most recognized high-style fundraisers in the nation. It raises funds for Care Resource, an AIDS social service agency in the Miami, Florida, area, which has one of the highest rates of AIDS in the nation. Tickets, which range from $150 to $529, include the party itself and a variety of other events that have expanded the fundraiser into a week-long event.

Held on the grounds of the historic Vizcaya mansion in Miami, everything is white—the tent, the dishes, the guests' outfits, and, of course, the serving staff uniforms. If the service staff dressed in the standard black and white, it would ruin the effect. Dressed all in white, they become virtually invisible.

While such an extra expense is probably out of the range of most groups, this organization can afford spectacular decorations because area businesses, restaurants, and bars donate most of the food and drink. Bars and restaurants provide service staff and all liquor is donated, either by the bar or a liquor company. Regional distributors are particularly inclined to do this when promoting a new brand or series of seasonal drinks.

LOOK TO THE EXPERTS

When choosing a menu, let the experts help. Banquet managers or caterers design several meals a day for many types of occasions. The group can benefit from their experience and advice. Keep in mind that these are only suggestions, and the group can modify them according to members' tastes and budget. In doing so, however, remember that these people regularly deal with large groups and know how to meet their needs.

GOING IT ALONE

For those who choose to forego the experts, it is possible for members to produce and serve a meal themselves. However, do not even consider this option unless there is a large group of culinarily inclined volunteers willing to pitch in.

First figure out how much food to buy, shop for it, find a place to cook it, prepare it, serve it, and clean it up. Items that will need to be rented include dishes, tablecloths, silverware, and often the serving ovens and other related equipment. Volunteers will be needed to set everything up and make sure it all gets back to the right place afterward.

Count on this route being very labor-intensive. Don't try it without firm commitments from a good-sized group of seasoned volunteers.

Think about balance among the foods while planning the menu. For a Mexican night, provide both spicy and mild dishes. At a Japanese dinner, not everyone will eat sushi, so offer a plainly prepared fish with choice of sauces for those who prefer their food cooked.

Besides appealing to a broad range of tastes, there are visual and textural facets to consider. Try to design each course so that there is a variety of color and texture.

Before finalizing the menu and shopping for supplies, analyze the limitations. How extensive a kitchen will be available? How much help and equipment will there be? How many electrical outlets are there and where are they? How skilled is the cooking staff? It is not a good idea to attempt something that is labor- and space-intensive, such as paella, if it must be produced in a home kitchen. Choose recipes that are as simple as possible and use the least equipment possible. If a recipe calls for stirring until something boils, someone will wind up stirring for ages waiting for a big pot to boil. And don't plan to have fresh vegetables such as string beans or mushrooms, which require painstaking cutting or cleaning. If the first and second courses need to be served hot, make sure there are enough burners and room to heat them both on the stove at once.

Will everything fit into the oven that needs to be in there at once? And what about refrigerator and freezer space? Will all perishable goods fit in? Once there's a tentative menu, hold a tasting, just as hotels and caterers do. Involve everyone who will be cooking. Try out all the recipes. This small-scale version of the meal will help the group work out problems that might not otherwise have been anticipated.

> **TIP** *Pay attention to the seasonality of some foods. Peaches may be a bargain when trying out a menu in July, but astronomically expensive in October—if they are available at all.*

After finalizing the menu, go through each recipe and list all the ingredients required. Don't forget cleaning supplies, paper towels, sponges, dishwashing liquid, garbage bags, etc. Figure out what is already available and how to arrange getting everything to the event site.

Next, prepare a shopping list. Do the multiplication at home, not in the supermarket aisles. For example, for a sit-down dinner, figure on six to eight ounces of protein (beef, fish, chicken, tofu, etc.) per person, a bit less for banquets. There are exceptions to this rule. If the group is feeding athletes who have just competed or the event includes a dance contest, expect heartier appetites. If the event is lengthy and dinner will not be served until the end, consider providing a snack early in the schedule.

Take recipes along to shop. Shop systematically, using a calculator to double-check figures. When possible, go to a food co-op or wholesale store such as Costco, BJ's, or Sam's Club to purchase supplies. Look for sales. Ask the manager whether there's a discount for large-quantity purchases. If there's more food to transport than one person can handle, arrange to have two or more people meet at the supermarket. If there is a store that's open 24 hours a day, go when it is quiet so the group members and their six shopping carts do not become a logistical nightmare. Don't buy perishables more than a few days before the event.

> **TIP** *When preparing food, liability is an important consideration should any of the items spoil. The more cooks and varieties of storage, the more likely it is to occur. Get insurance for such potential disasters, such as fires or food-borne illnesses.*

Time-Savers

There are lots of time-savers available. Use as many as are feasible. Prepare soups and beverages in advance, using about a quarter of the liquid needed. Transfer to a pot (or pitcher, for drinks), then add the rest of the liquid. Transport them to the event site already cooled. Frozen pie crusts save time in both preparation and cleanup (no pie plates to wash). Presliced meats and breads and frozen vegetables all reduce preparation time.

> **TIP** *When possible, arrange for some food to be prepared in advance at the homes of the cooks. (Do this only with cooks whose kitchens are adequate to handle this kind of preparation, and who maintain high health standards.)*

At the Site

On the day of the event, bring in everything needed. If possible, have foods sliced and cleaned at people's homes before being transported to the event site. Post the menu, cooking schedule, and assignment of tasks in a central location where everyone can refer to them. Use the best cooks for the big jobs; let the less culinarily inclined wash dishes and cut fruits or vegetables.

> **TIP** *Place garbage cans and large heavy-duty trash bags around the kitchen and, if outdoors, all around the site of the event, so no one will have to go far to find one. This allows people to clean up as they go.*

Inquire in advance about how trash disposal is handled. Is the group expected to clean up the site and haul off the trash? Is there someone to call who will pick it up and what does that cost?

To cope with unexpected emergencies, arrange to have a volunteer carpenter, electrician, and plumber on site with tools and cell phones. Offer to let them hand out business cards to guests and give them a full-page ad in the program book. Another option: Raffle off two hours of service from each of the volunteers, giving them added exposure.

If possible, arrange for an emergency medical van and staff to be on hand as well.

IF DISASTER STRIKES

No matter how well the group planned and how experienced the cooks are, sometimes something goes wrong. Always have someone taste dishes before they are served. That way, few will taste the failures. But there will come a time when someone uses salt instead of sugar, cornstarch instead of flour, burns something beyond recognition, or simply drops it on the floor.

Step One: Stay calm.

Step Two: No matter how desperate the group is, don't serve it. Instead, send someone out for some extras to fill in. A few possibilities:

- Assorted cheese and crackers
- Pre-cooked meats (ham, salami, chicken, turkey) rolled into tubes (stuffed with cream cheese is optional)
- Pre-cut vegetable plates and dip
- Assorted fruits (apples, orange wedges, grape clusters)
- Quick-cooking rice or pasta
- Frozen vegetables (canned is not a suitable substitute)
- Breads or crackers, butter and jam, or cheese spread
- Trays of store-bought cookies and chocolates
- Assorted frozen yogurts and gourmet ice cream

LIQUOR AND OTHER BEVERAGES

First decide if alcohol will be served. Unless there's a cash bar, alcohol will be a major expense. If the group is holding the event somewhere other than a hotel and has to buy its own liquor, that means a considerable outlay of money. There also is the potential liability if someone gets intoxicated at the event, then has a car accident on the way home. More states allow victims and their families to sue not only the person who was intoxicated, but whoever served the liquor, the group that hired the bartender, and the group's board of directors.

When serving liquor, try to make sure people don't drink too much and that cabs are available for those who should not drive home. Have volunteers or paid staff serve as spotters, looking for those who have overindulged and need a ride home. Usually, the organization pays the taxi fare.

The selection of beverages is determined by the type of event, the ages of those attending, and the menu. At most fancy banquets, dances, and other such events for adults, alcohol is generally available, either at a cash bar or as wine served at the table. But it's also customary to offer nonalcoholic beers and light alcohol punches as well as wine coolers, spritzers, sodas, and fruit juices.

Hotels usually charge per drink or per bottle for beverages. Most hotels will not allow groups to bring in donated wine or champagne, or if they do, they are likely to charge a flat per-bottle corkage fee (it could be $2 to $6 for each bottle opened) or a percentage of the value of each bottle. Considering that hotels charge considerably more for wine than stores do, it may still be less expensive to pay the corkage fee.

Cash bars are common these days because they help limit intake and cut liquor costs. Cash bars also reduce the number of servers needed. Keep the cocktail hour short—they used to run about 90 minutes, but most groups limit them to 45 minutes or an hour. Skip the after-dinner drinks and bottles of wine on the table. Or close the bar once dinner starts (and count on hearing a lot of complaints).

At some events, certain drinks go with the food served and can be big moneymakers. A few examples: Beer at a chili festival, Chianti with a spaghetti dinner, margaritas with Mexican fare, mojitos with Cuban fare. It's generally acceptable to serve drinks, but do so in moderation. For example, at many sporting events, liquor service is halted at half-time. Don't forget to offer alcohol-free versions, too.

As previously mentioned, liquor is expensive, and this is a good reason to consider whether the group should serve it. A 200-person event, for example, will require at least 40 bottles of wine—a minimum of two bottles per table of ten. At $20 a bottle times two for 20 tables, wine alone could cost $800. If people want other alcoholic beverages, the hotel or caterer will probably charge $2.75 or more per drink. The average person drinks two drinks. At $2.75, that's another $1,000. Then add two bars, bartenders, and setups. That's another $300. Already, expenses are $2,100 for liquor (not including tax and gratuity)—more than $10.50 per person. A cash bar can substantially offset this cost. Charging $3 per drink covers the bulk of the cost of cocktails and wine.

Soft drinks are mandatory even when serving alcohol. A good selection includes both regular and sugar-free cola, lemon-lime sodas, ginger ale, and caffeine-free colas (in regular and sugar-free versions); plus iced tea, bottled water, and fruit juices. Other possibilities include fruit-juice spritzers, lemonade, fresh cider, milkshakes, and ice cream sodas. Coffee and tea (regular and decaf for both) should be available, too. At outdoor events, especially when the weather is warm, make sure there is plenty of cold water available.

> **TIP** *Sometimes hotels will allow groups to bring in donated wine (although there's likely to be a corkage charge of as much as $10 a bottle for each bottle opened) and bottled waters if there's a cash bar. Caterers are more likely to let customers bring their own wine and liquor, because it's one less thing for them to worry about.*

How much coffee, soda, and alcohol are needed? The general rules of thumb for beverages are:

- Coffee: One pound makes about 60 cups.
- Champagne: One case pours 45 to 50 glasses.
- Liquor: One quart makes 25 to 30 drinks.
- Punch: One gallon makes 24 cups.

In terms of consumption, people generally drink less wine than beer, and less beer than soft drinks. For alcoholic drinks, figure about two drinks per person each hour. A few ways to cut beverage expenses include:

- Beer costs less in kegs than in bottles or cans. When possible (and practical), consider kegs. (They can be messy and slow, so they will not work well at all events, especially dressy ones.)

- When checking hard liquor prices, ask if the price is based on house brands (the cheapest), name or call brands (more expensive brands), or premium brands. Specify what brands to use and how much liquor should be poured per drink.

- Another option is to provide two drink tickets per paid guest. After that, guests pay for their own drinks.

- Specify that the charges be calculated based on the number of open bottles of liquor served.

When serving alcohol, keep in mind that there are legal issues to consider. Some states require a permit to hold an open bar. Serving liquor to minors is illegal. Doing so can cause legal trouble as well as draw disfavor from the public. And there are the previously mentioned issues of liability in connection with accidents that happen when guests leave the event. Know the local laws and obey them strictly.

FEEDING STAFF AND VOLUNTEERS

Try to arrange for workers to eat before they arrive at the event. It saves time, money, and effort. But if they are going to be there a long time (setting up or cleaning up), a meal will be necessary. At a hotel, ask if the chef could provide something simple, such as pasta and salad, in a room away from the event itself. Make sure there are beverages (coffee, soda, juice) available throughout the working period for anyone who is helping. It is cheaper if the group can provide these (bring them in ice chests), but some hotels don't allow it.

LEFTOVERS

Invariably, there is leftover food. With so many homeless and hungry people, try to make arrangements to donate leftovers to a soup kitchen or shelter. Hotels and caterers generally won't do this. It's up to the group to make arrangements. Plan on supplying containers and delivery. (Get a receipt from the charity for the donation.) It is a nice touch to mention this in the program or announce it at the event.

TIPPING

The general rule on tipping is that 18 percent is added on to the bill and divided accordingly: Fourteen percent to the waiters and bartenders, 3 percent to captains and maitre d's, 1 percent to the catering director. For exemplary service, feel free to tip as much as 22 percent.

If people really go out of their way to help with unexpected problems, give them something extra. If the service is excellent and the group hopes to hold another event there, give the maitre d'hotel or headwaiter something extra (about $100). Tip any particularly good waiters as well (about $50).

> **TIP** *Check to see if tax was included in the bill. Nonprofit organizations are exempt.*

Caution: Don't give these extra tips to the catering director to distribute, because the money may not get to the right people. Deliver them personally with a thank you to each recipient.

CHAPTER 8

Auctions and Other Profit Boosters

There's hardly an event held these days that can't boost profits by adding an auction to the lineup. With advances in computer software and the Internet combined with a population that's more computer savvy than ever, it's a fairly simple process to tailor an auction to both the event and the group's demographics.

Live auctions have long been combined with other events—fashion shows and dinner-dances, for instance—because they can produce serious money. The down side has been that live auctions can prove extremely labor-intensive to produce, with all that effort expended on a relatively small group in the hope that everyone will give generously. That formula can still work, provided the group has adequate manpower and resources.

Many organizations now elect to make the auction the main event, rather than an incidental add-on to some other activity. That's due, at least in part, to the aforementioned technological innovations of the past decade that have moved much of the action to cyberspace. As with so many other aspects of daily life, the Internet has vastly simplified the auction process and broadened the potential reach of even the smallest organizations. Some groups have switched entirely to online auction events. Others still want live gatherings that allow for the party and social interaction not possible on the Internet. And some groups use a combination of the two. Let's look at them one at a time.

INTERNET AUCTIONS

eBay, the ubiquitous online auction house, runs eBay Giving Works. It's a program through which charities can profit from access to eBay's 137 million customers. And profit they do. In a matter of a few years, the program has raised about $40 million for 8,800 charities.

The process provides two ways for charities to benefit: one for individuals wishing to donate to charities and another for charitable organizations seeking donations. Here's how it works: The organization signs up with MissionFish (www.missionfish.org) a nonprofit fundraising partner of eBay, which handles tracking and record-keeping of eBay items bought and sold for charity. Nonprofits must provide:

- A working e-mail address
- An electronic copy of the organization's logo
- A brief (40-word) mission statement
- A voided organization check
- Proof that it is tax exempt in the view of the Internal Revenue Service. (Schools, churches, and charitable groups qualify, but homeowners' associations and political action committees do not.)

There's no fee to register and the group gets listed in the eBay Giving Works online directory.

For individuals: When individual sellers use eBay, they specify what percentage of the sale of each item they wish to go to a specific nonprofit organization. Those items' listings on eBay carry a Giving Works ribbon icon that lets bidders know that a portion of the purchase price will benefit a charity. The name of the nonprofit group and the donation percentage appear in the item description. Bidding commences. (Nonprofits may cancel items listed on their behalf if they consider them unsuitable to the group's cause.)

When bidding ends, the seller sends the item to the buyer, as usual. Then MissionFish notifies the seller via e-mail the amount due the charity. The seller has two weeks to send in the donation. If the money doesn't arrive by then, MissionFish takes over, charging the seller's credit card, which it keeps on file. Then it sends the money to the charity and supplies the seller with a tax receipt. The company charges $3 (for operating expenses) plus 2.9 percent of the donation (for credit card processing charges).

For example, if an item sells for $1,000 and the seller pledged 50 percent to the charity, MissionFish divides the total in half, deducts its $3 service fee and 2.9 percent credit card charge (amounting to $14.50), and the nonprofit nets $482.50. Out of the seller's remaining $500, eBay receives its fees of about $31 and the seller nets $469. (In late 2006, eBay implemented its eBay Giving Works Fee Credit Policy, through which it now credits a portion of its fees equaling the percentage of the sales price the seller elected to donate to the nonprofit. See www.missionfish.org for details.)

> **TIP** *Once the group has registered and is listed in the Giving Works directory, let all the group's supporters know by e-mail, snail mail, and on the charity's Web site about the program and how they can use it to raise money for the charity. Consider holding training sessions so people will feel more confident using it and make sure to train plenty of people so they can assist others.*

For groups: Qualified organizations may post items as well, putting up in-kind gifts and donated items for bid in what basically comprises an on-line rummage sale. Rather than receiving the money through MissionFish, groups handle sales on their own behalf, collect the money themselves, and so pay no fee. The nonprofit lists the items for sale on eBay, and those items appear with the eBay Giving Works icon, the group's logo, its mission, and the fact that it will receive 100 percent of the final sale price. When bidding closes, the group collects the money and ships the items to the buyers.

So, if an item sells for $100 when a charity sells it directly, MissionFish and eBay waive their fees and the nonprofit gets all $100.

This sort of fundraising may seem more impersonal than a live event but "you can do a garage sale online and you, the nonprofit, don't have to deal with all the in-kind stuff," says Clam Lorenz, MissionFish's director of operations.

No one has to lug it all out to a specific spot at a specific time on a specific day. No one need worry about what the weather will be like. Instead, the group can accumulate all the items in a rented storage space (or a member's secure garage) as pieces are donated while people bid online. Once the bidding closes, the group collects payment from the buyers and ships their items. Any leftovers can be saved for another online sale, donated to some other charity, or sent to the group's thrift store, if it has one.

> **TIP** *Don't forget to include the shipping costs when selling online. The amount should be listed with the item so people can factor that into their bidding.*

This is an ideal way for a small local charity to tap into the worldwide appetite for Internet auctions. "Buyers prefer to buy items that benefit nonprofits," Lorenz says. "The items get more bids, are more likely to sell and sell for more money than the exact items on eBay that are not for charity. It makes the buyer feel good."

All sorts of charities raise money this way. *US Weekly* magazine, for example, held a Young Hot Hollywood 20 Celebrity Photo Auction in the fall of 2005. The entertainment magazine named the Young Hot Hollywood 20 stars and produced an awards show featuring them. At the event, the magazine asked stars such as Hilary Duff, Christina Aguilera, and Donald Trump to pose for portraits. The autographed photos went on the block on eBay and all the money raised from sales went toward Hurricane Katrina relief.

Of course, there's no precise way to predict which items will attract generous bidders—or that the items will sell at all. But, on the other hand, the group hasn't spent much trying it out.

One online auction item that raised close to $1 million in just two offerings over two years: lunch with mega-billionaire investor Warren Buffett. His late wife worked with The Glide Foundation, which provides social services to the poor and homeless in San Francisco. Every year since 2000, he has agreed to have lunch with the highest bidder on eBay and seven of that person's friends. The successful bidder anted up $351,100 in 2005. In 2006, just as Buffett pledged $30.7 billion of his $44 billion fortune to the Bill and Melinda Gates Foundation, the lunch went for $620,100.

Obviously, not everyone can land someone with Buffett's profit potential, but it illustrates how effective the Internet can be in raising money for charities with little effort and expense on the part of the charity. Even if a nationally known person isn't available, groups can ask popular local figures to offer a similar deal.

Both eBay (givingworks.ebay.com) and MissionFish (www.missionfish .org) provide extensive information and easy-to-follow instructions for getting started.

Live and virtual: Some groups may want to draw upon the best of both worlds and hold a combination event—both online and in person. Take the example of Hazel Wolf High School in Seattle, Wash., which appears as a successful case study on the MissionFish Web site.

The small private school had held a live auction annually for four years but, in 2004, decided to try the online route. Knowing the concept would be new to many people, the auction chairpeople (two parents who were volunteers) wrote letters to supporters explaining how the online auction would work and how to approach businesses for donations. More than two dozen students and their families solicited donations, amassing some 200 items in six weeks.

Because most of the packages and services donated were locally based, the group went all out letting the local online community know about it, sending letters and e-mails to school supporters, urging them, in turn, to notify friends and family.

To make sure that they didn't lose the social component people enjoyed at previous auctions, the group also had two bidding parties, where people could enjoy cocktails, hors d'oeuvres, and online bidding at computers set up for that purpose. This helped less confident online shoppers register for eBay accounts and go through the bidding process. The auction raised close to $10,000.

After the bidding concluded, the chair hosted a shipping party, inviting volunteers to spend the evening packaging items and writing thank-you notes. The group started brainstorming for the following year's auction while they were at it.

> **TIP** *Before launching a full-scale online auction, test the waters by offering just a few items to see how well the process works for the group.*

Exclusively virtual: Some charities choose to have closed-market auctions, in which auction companies put together an online event tailored to that charity's donors. The auction company supplies the charity with the tools needed to create its Internet auction page and to let donors know about it by e-mail. Closed-market auctions are generally less competitive than a site such as eBay and allow charities to keep their donors to themselves. Among the companies that orchestrate closed-market auctions are cMarket (cmarket.com) and Benefit Events (www.BenefitEvents.com). Even internationally known companies such as Christie's (www.christies.com) and Sotheby's (www.sothebys.com) auction off items for charities, often charging them a lower fee.

UP CLOSE AND PERSONAL

There are still those times when only a live auction will do. Although they require significantly more effort by a greater number of people than the online variety, there are situations in which these still raise substantial amounts when handled well by people passionately committed to a cause.

That's what drives the success of the Naples Winter Wine Festival, held each winter in Naples, Florida. It began in 2001, when a group of wealthy friends came up with a way to combine their love of food and wine with their desire to give back to the community.

The weekend commences Friday morning with a visit to some of the 18 children's charities the wine auctions help fund. Seeing the struggles of low-income families, many of whom belong to the large service industry upon which the city's affluent population relies, brings home the difference between the lives of beneficiaries and the donors, shows donors how their money is spent, and generally spurs more generous giving.

Many of the 18 founding couples were extremely well connected—and extremely persistent—and they cajoled some of the nation's top chefs and vintners to converge on Naples for a long winter weekend. Among the renowned chefs successfully lured to the event have been Thomas Keller, Emeril Lagasse, Charlie Trotter, and Todd English.

On Friday night, there are lavish dinners at the founders' private estates, with a celebrity chef and vintner teaming up at each home. On Saturday, the grand auction takes place at The Ritz-Carlton Golf Resort in Naples. Although extremely rare and expensive wines are the auction stars, the festival organizers reel in other eye-popping donations, including trips for four to the Cannes Film Festival. At the 2005 auction, one couple spent $340,000 for a blue Maserati that carried a ticket price of $113,005.

Rather than trying to attract the greatest number of people possible, the group limits sales to 550 tickets, issuing invitations first to those who were big spenders in previous years. People pay between $3,500 and $5,000 each to attend. Many also spend well into the six figures on auction items. In 2006, the event raised close to $14 million, making it the most successful charity wine event in the world for the third consecutive year.

For the 2007 festival, the group has added a Thursday night wine tasting with internationally acclaimed wine critic Robert Parker, Jr. Those who choose to attend will pay $12,500 per person for the privilege, in addition to the standard ticket price for the rest of the event.

Sure, this is an extreme example. Few events could raise that much money in one long weekend. Nonetheless, groups with organized, motivated workers can create extremely lucrative live events.

> **TIP** *Make sure that items offered for auction match the income level of the people who attend.*

While it still takes a concerted effort to acquire alluring items and make sure people turn out to bid on them, much of the time-consuming record-keeping and tracking has been substantially reduced with the advent of event software programs.

Auctionpay (www.auctionpay.com) is a leader in the field, providing payment processing software specifically designed for benefit auctions. The company's software can streamline the paperwork that often bogs down an event.

It was just such confusing registration and long checkout lines at charity auctions that frustrated Jeff Jetton so much he created Auctionpay as a means of simplifying the check-in and check-out processes.

He started with a program that preloads customers' account information. Then at checkout, it takes no time at all to pay for the item purchased. From there, the company added event management software that helps track donated items, assign seats, and make note of guests' food preferences.

Purchasing the required software may constitute a significant expense for many groups—the complete Auctionpay event suite package runs about

$2,000 including set up and licensing fees—but it's likely to pay for itself through repeated use and savings on such items as catalogs, bid sheets, customized receipts, procurement, and thank-you letters. It can help with the planning and execution of other sorts of benefit events.

It also allows people to register and pay for the event online. And, most importantly, they can donate the same way throughout the year.

Auctionpay launched another program for nonprofits in July 2006 called Auction Booster, says Peter Hoogerhuis, Auctionpay vice president of marketing. "It provides packages we've procured for nonprofits—travel packages, airfare, hotels, etc. We provide them at very good prices to nonprofits, they mark them up and sell them."

The advantage is that the charity doesn't buy the packages ahead of time. People reserve the packages at the event, then the charity orders them through Auctionpay.

"We find a lot of people who will look at these and smaller auctions won't have the resources to procure them or buy them," Hoogerhuis says. "It adds a level of excitement and high-end capability to the whole auction event."

The goal of the Auctionpay package is "to make it nice and efficient and to enhance the guest experience," Hoogerhuis says. "Registration is easy, buying items and checking out are easy and fast. It reduces the workload on volunteers, helps in the procurement and after the event there's no having to go back to each donor to provide a letter with tax details. Ultimately, it makes for a better experience, which means donors will be coming back and hopefully you'll increase the funds raised at the next event."

Beyond the practical concerns, Hoogerhuis says that baby boomers and younger adults expect a savvy charity to have such tools. They will expect to be able to handle most of their business online and may limit their support to those charities that allow them to do this.

Emerging technology saves time and energy, but it will not make an auction—or any other event, for that matter—a success on its own.

Groups must still make the event enjoyable in other ways, such as having it at an appealing (but affordable) setting, providing quality cocktails and food, employing a skilled auctioneer (it's worth spending the money if no one can find one willing to donate services), and making sure bidding doesn't drag on and lose momentum. It should not be a test of endurance. If necessary, break the live auction in half, with less expensive items going early on and the more sought-after, higher-priced ones offered later, after guests have had some food and drinks.

One strategy that helps ease the last-minute crunch of people trying to pay for items and leave is to shut down bidding at different tables at different times. If items are sorted by type, it's easy for people to shop. Then, as the event progresses, organizers can close bidding on the table with spa services and jewelry certificates, for example. This allows those tallying up the bids to do so in smaller chunks and guests can continue bidding on items at tables that remain open.

Also remember that sometimes less is more, as the organizers of the 17th annual Culinary Evening with the California Winemasters discovered. The group raised $1.29 million for the Cystic Fibrosis Foundation, setting a new record for the event, according to *Wine Spectator's* July 31, 2006 issue. For the first time, they limited the number of live auction lots to keep the excitement level high and expanded the silent auction items so there was still plenty on which to bid.

> **TIP** *When creating invitations for an event that will include an auction, include a card that lists some of the most desirable items. It's also possible to set a "Buy it Now" price for those who don't wish to wait for the auction, won't be able to attend, or don't mind spending more for the immediate gratification. If the auction will be accessible online, include that information, too, so that even those who can't attend can take part.*

Auctions surely occupy the highest rung of the profit ladder, but there are some other strategies groups can employ in addition to, or instead of, an auction, including the following.

ADVERTISING

Sell advertising at the event, just as the sports and race car teams do. Sell the space on the walls, doors, and tables. Sponsors can purchase one or all three. The company's name gets displayed at each table on a balloon bouquet or on the table assignment cards guests pick up at registration. Sponsors can hand out coupons to promote their products. These can either be placed on tables or in goody bags guests receive on their way out.

Balloons

Have volunteers walk around offering helium-filled balloons for sale. Each one contains a number corresponding to a gift (which committee members have gotten donated with donors' names and business logos prominently displayed in the room).

Set prices at about a third to half the cost of the prizes (if the prize is a $40 dinner for two, balloons should sell for about $20). Because the value of the gift is guaranteed to be more than the balloon costs, people are more likely to buy them. Among the items that motivate buyers are certificates good for rounds of golf, ski tickets, facials, massages, manicures, dinners, and gourmet chocolates.

Duck Pond/Grab Bag

The game is just what the name indicates. Buy or borrow an inexpensive kiddy pool, fill it with water, and get some rubber ducks to bob about. Put numbers on their bellies in waterproof ink before setting the quackers loose. People buy a duck and get a prize that corresponds to the number on that duck.

Or try a race course—a sliding board that empties into the pool, for example. People bet on a numbered duck, then all set off from the top of the sliding board. Water coursing down the board will wash the competitors down to the pond. The first duck to make a splash wins a prize for the person who bet on it.

Dunk Tank

If the activity is a casual one at which a little mess won't be a problem, line up some local personalities and/or politicians for a dunk tank. Guests pay to pitch a ball at the lever that drops dunkees into a tank of water.

Guess How Many

Get a big jar, and fill it with jellybeans, coins, marbles, shells, etc. Or fill a treasure chest with money and charge people to guess how much is in there. Another variation: Get a huge vegetable and have people guess how much it weighs without picking it up. Naturally, someone overseeing the competition needs to know the answer ahead of time. At the end of the event, reveal the answer and pick a winner from all the correct entries.

If there are only a couple that got it right, split the winnings. This is a good addition to festivals and other outdoor events and takes little preparation or manpower.

Key Club

Sell keys that correspond to locks on donated prizes. Sell keys for bicycles, cars, boats, personal watercraft, motorcycles, or even items that don't normally have locks. Not everyone will win in this game.

Mini-Auction

Hold a brief auction at a ball, dinner, or food and wine event. Get five or six big-ticket items (donated, of course) and auction them off. Auction the table centerpieces, too. Keep this to 15 minutes or so or it can ruin the flow of the evening. Don't do it too early, either. People tend to be more generous once they've gotten into the spirit—and perhaps had a drink or two.

Program Book

These can be hugely profitable. Be prepared to provide potential advertisers with printed information about how many books the group plans to distribute, some details on the organization's mission, and the demographics of those who are expected to attend (see Exhibit 8.1). Sell ads of varying sizes—business-card size (10 to a page), eighth-, quarter-, half-, and whole-page ads. For bigger-budget advertisers, sell a whole page in platinum or silver and use that color paper for those pages. Glossy metallic sheets of gold and silver paper are readily available.

> **TIP** *If the event has been held at least once already, give volunteers a sample of the previous year's book to show when selling the current year. This helps potential advertisers understand what the group does, and allows them to see what various size ads look like. If this is the group's first try at a program book, have those selling it take along sheets that show the various sizes of ads available. Don't forget that a lot of business-card-sized ads can quickly add up.*

Meals on Wheels Delaware became so successful in gathering silent auction items that it could no longer use its $5\frac{1}{2}$- by $8\frac{1}{2}$-inch program book for

EXHIBIT 8.1 HIRSCHFELD RATES

© AL HIRSCHFELD. ART REPRODUCED BY SPECIAL ARRANGEMENT
WITH HIRSCHFELD'S EXCLUSIVE REPRESENTATIVE,
THE MARGO FEIDEN GALLERIES LTD., NEW YORK.

HIRSCHFELD

The Artwork of Al Hirschfeld

May 2-June 5, 1999

FACT SHEET

Opening Preview: Sunday, May 2, 1999 • 5:00-8:00 pm

Exhibit Date: Monday, May 3-Saturday, June 5, 1999 (Exhibit extension through summer possible)

Presented by: Jewish Community Centers of Greater Philadelphia and the Prince Music Theater, a new home, a new name for the American Music Theater Festival; and the Margo Feiden Galleries, Ltd., New York (Hirschfeld's exclusive representative)

Where: In the Borowsky Gallery at the Gershman Y on Broad and Pine Streets, Philadelphia

What: The celebrated line drawings of Al Hirschfeld, the finest caricaturist of our time, will be on display at the Borowsky Gallery at the Gershman Y, in conjunction with the opening of The Prince Music Theater, the new home of the American Music Theater Festival.

For the first time in Philadelphia history, Hirschfeld's drawings will be on display and on sale in one exhibit. Exhibit will emphasize celebrity drawings from the world of theater and film, particularly those who once appeared in Philadelphia. Hirschfeld's drawings of celebrated actors, actresses and entertainers, have been displayed around the world and featured in *The New York Times* and on the covers of *Time* and *TV Guide*. This summer, come see why Hirschfeld has been called "The Line King" of Broadway.

Editorial Support: The Al Hirschfeld retrospective exhibit will receive substantial and media placement, courtesy of daily and community publications as well as television and radio stations.

Local Publications:
The Philadelphia Inquirer
Philadelphia Daily News
Jewish Exponent
Ritz Filmbill
City Paper

Philadelphia Weekly
Daily Pennsylvanian
WXPN-FM
WHYY
Philadelphia Online & Other Websites

Sponsors:

For information contact Jessica Resnick at (215) 446-3002

EXHIBIT 8.1   CONTINUED

© AL HIRSCHFELD. ART REPRODUCED BY SPECIAL ARRANGEMENT
WITH HIRSCHFELD'S EXCLUSIVE REPRESENTATIVE,
THE MARGO FEIDEN GALLERIES LTD., NEW YORK.

The
Artwork of
Al Hirschfeld

May 2-June 5, 1999

Corporate and Individual Sponsorship Benefits

$50,000 Title Sponsor

- NAME RECOGNITION as "The Artwork of Al Hirschfeld" title sponsor
- Your CORPORATE LOGO and/or COMPANY NAME on all printed materials and media for the exhibit including the flag on the Avenue of the Arts lamp post in front of the Gershman Y
- PRIVATE RECEPTION for your company during the exhibit
- BACK OUTSIDE COVER of the collectable exhibit catalogue

- YOUR OWN COMMISSIONED HIRSCHFELD IMAGE
- Opportunity to present CORPORATE MATERIALS and/or PROMOTIONAL ITEMS during the length of the exhibit
- 26 TICKETS to the Opening night reception on May 2, 1999
- 100 VIP PASSES to exhibit
- Discount coupons to the Prince Music Theater Series

$25,000 Presenting Sponsor

- NAME RECOGNITION as "The Artwork of Al Hirschfeld" presenting sponsor
- Your CORPORATE LOGO and/or COMPANY NAME on all printed materials and media for the exhibit
- INSIDE COVER of the collectable exhibit catalogue
- PRIVATE RECEPTION

- Opportunity to present CORPORATE MATERIALS and/or PROMOTIONAL ITEMS during the length of the exhibit
- 14 TICKETS to the Opening night reception on May 2, 1999
- 50 VIP PASSES to exhibit
- Discount coupons to the Prince Music Theater Series

$15,000 Grand Benefactor

- NAME RECOGNITION as "The Artwork of Al Hirschfeld" grand benefactor
- Your CORPORATE LOGO and/or COMPANY NAME on all printed materials and media for the exhibit
- FULL PAGE AD in the collectable exhibit catalogue
- PRIVATE RECEPTION

- Opportunity to present CORPORATE MATERIALS and/or PROMOTIONAL ITEMS during the length of the exhibit
- 6 TICKETS to the Opening night reception on May 2, 1999
- 30 VIP PASSES to exhibit
- Discount coupons to the Prince Music Theater Series

$5,000 Benefactor

- Your CORPORATE LOGO and/or COMPANY NAME on all printed materials and media for the exhibit
- HALF PAGE AD in the collectable exhibit catalogue

- 4 TICKETS to the Opening night reception on May 2, 1999
- 20 VIP PASSES to exhibit
- Discount coupons to the Prince Music Theater Series

$2,500 Patron

- Your CORPORATE LOGO and/or COMPANY NAME on all printed materials and media for the exhibit
- QUARTER PAGE AD in the collectable exhibit catalogue

- 2 TICKETS to the Opening night reception on May 2, 1999
- 10 VIP PASSES to exhibit
- Discount coupons to the Prince Music Theater Series

For sponsorship information or questions contact Jessica Resnick at (215) 446-3002

(continues)

EXHIBIT 8.1 CONTINUED

HIRSCHFELD

The Artwork of Al Hirschfeld

May 2-June 5, 1999

© AL HIRSCHFELD. ART REPRODUCED BY SPECIAL ARRANGEMENT WITH HIRSCHFELD'S EXCLUSIVE REPRESENTATIVE, THE MARGO FEIDEN GALLERIES LTD., NEW YORK.

• • *Exhibit Catalogue Advertising Form** • •

I hereby authorize the following ad to be placed in the Hirschfeld Exhibit Catalogue in the size indicated below:

Ad Size	Dimensions	Cost
Inside Covers (Front or Back)	7 1/2 x 10 (no bleeds)	$1,000
• 10 Opening night reception tickets and 10 VIP Passes to the exhibit		
Full Page	7 1/2 x 10	$750
• 8 Opening night reception tickets and 10 VIP Passes to the exhibit		
Half Page	7 1/2 x 5 (h)	$500
• 6 Opening night reception tickets and 10 VIP Passes to the exhibit		
Quarter Page	3 3/4 x 5 (v)	$250
• 4 Opening night reception tickets and 10 VIP Passes to the exhibit		
Eighth Page	3 3/4 x 2 1/2 (h)	$100
• 2 Opening night reception tickets and 10 VIP Passes to the exhibit		

Please furnish CAMERA-READY copy for all ads or call the JCCs of Greater Philadelphia to arrange for copy to be typeset. All ads MUST be designed to exact ad size purchased or they will be reset to fit.
See reverse for guidelines for camera-ready art.

Payment MUST Accompany space reservation.
PLEASE MAKE CHECKS PAYABLE TO and send to
JCCs of Greater Philadelphia • 401 S. Broad St., Phila., PA 19147 attn: Jessica Resnick
Special positions sold on a first come, first served basis.

This contract must be returned WITH CAMERA-READY COPY or copy instructions by _____

Name of Company or Individual: _____

Contact Name: _____

Address: _____

City: _____ State: _____ Zip: _____

Phone: _____

Signature: _____ Date: _____

The above ad is 100% tax deductible, as provided by law, either as a business advertising expense or a charitable contribution.
Your support is greatly appreciated.

Questions? Call Jessica Resnick at (215) 545-4400, ext. 3002
JCCs of Greater Philadelphia • 401 South Broad Street • Philadelphia, PA 19147

*Based on sponsorship level, some advertising is included.
A branch of the Jewish Community Centers of Greater Philadelphia and a constituent agency of the Jewish Federation of Greater Philadelphia.
In partnership with the Prince Music Theater, a new home, a new name for the American Music Theater Festival.

EXHIBIT 8.1 CONTINUED

Hirschfeld Catalog Ad Sizes

Inside Covers (Front or Back)
7 1/2 x 10 (no bleeds)
$1,000

Full Page
7 1/2 x 10
$750

Half Page   7 1/2 x 5 (h)
$500

Quarter Page
3 3/4 x 5 (v)
$250

Eighth Page   3 3/4 x 2 1/2 (h)
$100

its annual auction. The event was part of a three-day event called "Weekend with the Masters." It includes dinners by guest chefs hosted by local restaurants, an evening event with rotating cooking demonstrations by the celebrity chefs, and Sunday's Celebrity Chef's Brunch, featuring 30 top chefs from around the country, each with an individual food station.

In lieu of a program book, the group sets up tables with items grouped according to type. Next to each item is a laminated card that describes the item, as would generally appear in a program book. The group also hangs large signs from the ceiling that indicate which types of items are immediately below and they hand out maps that help guest navigate the auction area as well as the food and beverage sections.

By freeing them of a program book to tote around, guests can hold a drink or small plate of food and still have a hand free to place bids. There are also lots of staff around ready to relieve guests of empty dishes and glasses so they need not step away from the silent auction items.

What, no program book?

As guests depart, they get a goodie bag that includes a magazine-style cookbook that features the participating chefs and some of their recipes (see Exhibit 8.2). It also has lot of ads, a full explanation of what the group does, and informs readers that Meals on Wheels Delaware serves 600,000 meals a year to homebound seniors around the state. Unlike program books, which are likely to be discarded at or right after the event, the cookbooks become mementos people save from year to year, giving the charity's sponsors even more exposure.

The cookbooks, unlike standard programs, have lasting value and so those remaining can be sold after the event, adding still more income.

In creating a program book, cookbook, or any sort of publication in which space will be sold, set rates according to size and placement. The premier spot, the back page, commands the highest price, say $3,000. Inside covers should sell for $2,500. Then stack the advertising options so there's something in every price range down to a basic listing for $25.

If someone in the group is adept at desktop publishing (and many people are these days), the group can save a lot of money by producing its own book. Try to secure underwriting to cover printing costs.

If they are small and compact, give out program books as guests arrive. They should contain a description of the program, an easy-to-digest primer on the organization and its goals, pictures from past events, a list of com-

EXHIBIT 8.2 MEALS FROM THE MASTERS CELEBRITY CHEFS' BRUNCH COMMEMORATIVE COOKBOOK

mittee members, appropriate tribute to sponsors, perhaps a letter of support from a political bigwig, and as many ads as the committees can sell.

TIP *Letters from and pictures of those who have benefited from the charity's work can serve as powerful motivators in making people dig deeper into their wallets.*

Raffle/Door Prizes

It's common these days to include raffle tickets in invitations. This encourages advance purchases and helps involve people who might not otherwise attend. They might not buy a $250 ticket to a formal dinner/dance, but they might spring for $25 in raffle tickets on a chance to win a cruise or spa package. (The winner need not be present to win.)

> **TIP** When crafting the invitations, make sure there's a spot on the response card that allows those invited to purchase raffle tickets even if they can't attend. Include the tickets in the envelope. People can mail back the stubs with their payment if they don't attend or bring the stubs with them if they do. Make sure to track tickets by recording the numbers and who they are sent to before mailing them out. This can be done by hand or with an Excel spreadsheet.

Sell additional raffle tickets during the event. Display the prizes (sporting equipment, cases of beer or wine, gift baskets, cruise posters, etc.). Or hold a 50/50 raffle: Someone wins half the money collected and the charity keeps the other half. This type of raffle is very popular at big events such as festivals.

CHAPTER 9

Reaching for the Stars

There's no question that hitching a special event to a big-name star can attract attention to the cause and raise serious money. However, consider the other possible outcome: It can also spark a disaster of stellar proportions. Before deciding to tackle a celebrity event, consider the myriad hidden costs and requirements that come with it. While it's possible it will be worth the extra effort, keep in mind that star power can create magic—or a black hole where the budget used to be.

WHEN FREE COSTS MONEY

Many celebrities are generous with their time and will agree to appear at a charitable event without charge. For a big-name star, that might mean a savings of $100,000 or more. Or does it? If the entertainment involves a professional athlete signing autographs, a comic doing standup, or a political pundit sounding forth, the logistics will be far simpler and the costs considerably less than bringing in a singer or dancer. The star may not charge for appearing, but the charity still will have to pay her 10-piece band to rehearse and perform (at $50 to $100 an hour per musician), not to mention transporting, housing, and feeding everyone.

Then add in the costs of staging, lighting, sets, and props. That "free" entertainment can wind up costing thousands of dollars. Again, look at the celebrity's contract. It will contain a rider, which is a list of requirements for producing the show.

Those who have never planned a complicated celebrity concert before should spend the $500 or so to have an attorney look over the contract. It could save thousands of dollars later. Consider that stars normally have 20- to 30-page contracts, with riders listing their individual requirements for appearance. Each star's contract also includes such things as the manner in which they must travel (usually first class); their accommodations (usually a suite); how many people travel in their entourage (anywhere from one to 30, including makeup artists, hairdressers, personal valets, musicians, tour managers, reiki masters, and psychics); the entourage's travel and lodging requirements; what meals must be provided and what foods should be served; cancellation clauses; and anything else the star requires. Make sure the attorney who examines the contract is familiar with entertainment and contract laws. Another option: Ask the business manager of a regional theater to review it.

LINING UP A CELEBRITY

If the group can afford to bring in a star (see Chapter 2, Money Matters, to calculate this), the next step is to decide if the time, energy, and trouble involved will pay off in the form of substantially more people attending the event and, presumably, donating more money. In most cases, the answer is yes, especially for first-time events or those competing with many others for attention.

The next step is to figure out what star will best suit the event. There are all sorts of celebrities—local sports stars and media personalities, politicians, chefs, artists, actors, authors, directors, singers, dancers. Obviously, it's easier to get local figures to appear at an event in their hometown, and also far less expensive because there will be no airfare or lodging required. However, those who want a national or international star should think about the nature of the event and whether the person they are considering fits the occasion and overall mission.

Besides the appropriateness of the celebrity, how much the group can afford to pay will be a primary limiting factor. An entertainment budget of $3,000 will not buy mega stars such as Jennifer Lopez, the cast of *Queer Eye for the Straight Guy*, or Kanye West. If the event is a sports celebrity auction, for example, a modest budget may allow for the appearance of a local sports or media personality to serve as auctioneer. Then ask various sporting goods stores or teams for donations of jerseys, hats, balls, tickets, and so on. More and more local celebrities, including sports figures, command fees of as much as $10,000 for appearances, autograph signings, and endorsements.

Musical acts, such as Itzhak Perlman or Bernadette Peters, can cost from $55,000 to $200,000 (add $5,000 or more for the travel expenses of staff and key musicians). Comedians such as Robin Williams, Billy Crystal, Chris Rock, and Ellen Degeneres can cost within the same range, but with lower staff travel expense. For stars such as Donald Trump, Jerry Seinfeld, or Oprah Winfrey, the figures climb exponentially.

For groups hoping to bring in more than one celebrity with a tight entertainment budget, try to negotiate a "favored nations" clause. (A job for a lawyer.) This clause ensures that if two or more stars appear, all are treated equally. They are paid the same amount, and they get the same accommodations, amenities, and billing. Sometimes the group can negotiate a lower fee because the celebrities want to work together, or because it's a cause they support or they view it as good exposure for them.

> **TIP** *The organization can save money if someone else has already hired the star and provided transportation. If the star must stay longer for the group's event, the organization will then only be responsible for additional hotel expenses and possibly airfare home.*

SERIOUS STARGAZING

Lining up celebrities requires energy, persistence, and creativity. Groups most likely to convince them to appear are those in which they have a personal interest, if they are going to be in the area at the time of the event, and the organization can afford their fee (possibly through corporate underwriting).

So how to go about this? Start by watching television. Study the talk shows, entertainment news shows, and televised benefits. Stars frequently discuss their interests and upcoming schedules on *The Tonight Show, Entertainment Tonight,* and similar programs.

Read newspapers. Even the tabloids contain some news about celebrities and the causes they care about, although they may be hiding beneath the "Space aliens take over remote Texas town, balance budget" stories. Many newspapers have devoted substantial space to stories about Dionne Warwick, Elton John, Stevie Wonder, Gladys Knight, Elizabeth Taylor, and Sharon Stone, all of whom have taken active roles in AIDS-related fundraising because of the disease's devastating impact on the entertainment industry. Katie Couric, whose husband died of colon cancer, crusades for cancer screening and awareness. Doris Day is a passionate advocate for animal welfare. Sting has spent years promoting Amnesty International's mission. And, of course, Jerry Lewis is synonymous with the Muscular Dystrophy Association, whose telethon he hosts every year.

Don't forget to check out the Web sites of specific stars as well. Just about everybody who's anybody has an official site and it's likely to include a section about the star's favorite causes. Pamela Anderson's, for instance, has extensive information about the work she's done with People for the Ethical Treatment of Animals (including a photo of her wearing nothing but a sprinkling of snow—no naughty bits showing) and a caption that reads: "Give fur the cold shoulder." Oprah Winfrey's site includes pages on how to help capture child predators and another on the plight of women in Afghanistan. With the proliferation of Web sites, it's easier than ever to find out what causes stars care about.

The Greater Delaware Valley Chapter of the National Multiple Sclerosis Society held a highly successful and cost-effective celebrity event in Philadelphia when it put on "An Evening with Richard Cohen and Meredith Vieira: Living with MS – Impact on Families and Careers." Vieira, from television's hit show *The View*, and her Emmy-Award-winning author/director husband attracted a crowd of more than 1,000. Cohen was diagnosed with multiple sclerosis when he was 25 years old and wrote the book, *Blindsided: Lifting a Life Above Illness*, chronicling his 30-year battle with the disease and how it's affected his wife and three children.

The MS Society was able to offer free admission because Serono/Pfizer sponsored the program. This was a friend-raiser, rather than a fundraiser, but it's likely that many who attended will go on to contribute time, money, or both to the organization as a result.

Bringing in a big-name speaker can help charities raise money, too, as long as the person and the topic appeal to the target audience. And, although some speakers command six-figure fees to appear, there are many well-known personalities whose speaking fees may be affordable.

One place to start would be with a speakers' bureau, such as the Greater Talent Network in New York City. The agency represents a wide range of speakers—athletes and politicians, entrepreneurs and astronauts, actors, comedians, and authors. The network's senior vice president, Kenny Rahtz, serves as a matchmaker between the speakers and the charities.

"It's really about getting the appropriate celebrity and working very closely with the group to make sure the person they bring in is a magnetic draw, someone who has some connection, either personally or through family and friends, to the event," he said.

A speaker might help spark renewed interest in an event that's been held annually for several years and may have lost some of its appeal. Speakers can cost anywhere from $5,000 to $300,000 plus so it's helpful to have someone who can narrow down the possibilities. Once the charity picks a speaker, the network staff will help set up advance interviews with the media so the fundraising group's staff can attend to the many other tasks involved. If the group opts to have a series of speakers, the network can arrange that, too, saving the charity's staff and volunteers countless hours trying to round up likely candidates on their own.

The Internet can provide still more information about celebrities. Ticketmaster's site offers hundreds of listings detailing which stars are touring and where they will be. Local performing art centers and arenas have Web sites that list who will be coming and when. Check the Web sites of venues within a 500-mile radius of town. See who will be appearing at these facilities, and make a seasonal or year-long schedule of celebrities who will be in the vicinity. The costs are far smaller to bring in someone from a nearby city than from a distant coast. And make sure to check the celebrity's Web site. It generally offers information about the star and where the person will perform over the next few months or year.

An expensive but highly useful resource is Celebrity Service, which publishes a newsletter that details the projects and appearances of countless stars. The service runs several thousand dollars per year, but might be worth the investment for groups planning several events that might include celebrities. (See Chapter 13, Tools of the Trade.)

Another route is to consider having a speaker rather than a star-studded performance. As mentioned in Chapter 1, countless stars, athletes, news personalities, actors, and others are available through speakers' bureaus. This strategy route is far more straightforward and less involved than bringing in celebrities to perform.

HARNESSING STAR POWER

For the group whose organizers are determined to land a big star to perform, list all those who might be interested in the charity and might also be in the vicinity around the time of the event. Then it's time to invite them to appear. A group representative could take the usual route and call a booking agent. Don't. He is a middleman who generally makes 10 percent or more of the amount he books the celebrity for, and so is looking to get the highest appearance fee possible. The booking agent negotiates with the agency that represents the artist. The agency also gets a percentage, so the agent there will also want to get the highest amount possible. Then the agent from the representing agency goes to the star's personal manager, who also gets a percentage . . .

Get the picture?

Now there are three people between the organization and the celebrity, each of whom is interested in making as much money as possible. This route ensures the organization will pay top dollar.

It's possible and not all that difficult to reduce the number of middlemen. First, if someone in the organization knows the star, ask that person to explain to the celebrity the charitable cause and its mission. This works best if it's a charity in which the celebrity is interested.

"Unless the celebrity is really involved in the cause and has a personal reason to be there, I'd recommend not doing it," says Shelley Clark, vice president of Lou Hammond and Associates, Inc. in New York City. "You're not just buying someone's presence."

Charities seeking a price break will fare best by going through a celebrity's publicist. Most celebrities have a publicist, whose job it is to get the star media exposure. The publicist gets a standard retainer, rather than a percentage of the star's bookings. Celebrity Service lists the publicists, business managers (for legal and accounting matters), and agents that handle each star. But even for those who don't subscribe, there are ways to get to the star.

If a celebrity doesn't have a publicist but appears on a network television show, that show will have a publicist. Contact the television network and ask. The network publicist can usually help make contact with the celebrity's personal manager. All shows go on break for part of the year. Find out when that is and see if the star might be available to travel then.

That may seem a fairly straightforward process, but it's not. A star's personal manager is generally the toughest person to contact. Most rarely return calls to people they don't know. Persistence is often the key to getting through. Start calling well in advance, and always leave a message. Do not be rude. Politely let the person who answers know that someone from the organization will continue to call until the person reaches the personal manager. There is an organization of personal managers (see Chapter 13, Tools of the Trade) that maintains a membership list. Sometimes the star's agent can supply it.

For almost any celebrity, contact the union, the Screen Actors Guild (SAG) or the American Federation of Television and Radio Actors (AFTRA). (See Chapter 13, Tools of the Trade.) Both SAG and AFTRA have offices in New York or Los Angeles, and someone there can supply the name of the publicist or personal manager.

Having obtained the proper contact, make that call count. Persistence is more important than genius. It may take multiple calls to get through. As with personal managers, be polite. Just make it clear that someone will keep calling until they get to talk to a person who can give them an answer. Remember that publicists and managers may get as many as 500 calls a day, so there is only a minute or so to make the plea. Plan what to say. (Writing out a script is a good idea.) Make the pitch concise, and make it clear what's in it for the celebrity. Those who do their homework will mention why they know the person might want to help, and that they are in town (or nearby) the day of the event.

"It's not about flattery," says Shelley Clark. "I wouldn't even talk about how much publicity there will be. Get the fit out there. Give a sense of the event, the worthiness of the cause and why you think that cause would appeal to this particular celebrity."

After getting a verbal commitment, follow it up with a formal letter of agreement, or ask for a written contract.

Ask the star's publicist for a schedule of performances, then schedule the event around those dates. In New York City, for example, many charity events take place on Monday nights because Broadway actors are off then and thus are available for special appearances.

Just as important is to find out what dates to avoid. Don't schedule a sports event—or anything else, if possible—on a weekend when there's a big game. That would be a supreme waste of star power. And check to make sure the event won't fall on a religious holiday.

Getting a commitment that a star will appear is only half the battle. Making sure the contract doesn't leave the group vulnerable—or committed to spending money it doesn't have—is vital.

Thoroughly check the celebrity's standard contract, or have a lawyer do so. It should state that the celebrity is attending for free (or whatever the agreed upon price is) and who is paying for extras (travel, room, and food, including what will be provided for those traveling with the star). Be specific. For example, if the group does not plan to pay for long-distance phone calls, damaged hotel furniture, or room service, state this clearly in the written agreement, give a copy of the agreement to the hotel's front desk, and request that the general manager sign it.

Do the same thing with limousine companies. Make it clear what the charity will be responsible for, and stipulate that the limo should get cash or credit cards from their customers for anything beyond that. Some entertainers are infamous for taking advantage of charities this way.

Fundraisers unfamiliar with large-scale celebrity events can make very expensive mistakes. For example, a fundraiser new to such events cost his charity money by not getting the deal in writing with the management of a hotel at which a special event was held. A few weeks after the event, when the bills came in from the hotel, there was an additional bill from room service for $4,000 in champagne and caviar—charges racked up by the backup singers of the entertainer who performed at the event. The charity paid these unanticipated expenses out of the money raised that evening, rather than harass the celebrity, who had given an excellent performance and helped attract a sell-out crowd.

> **TIP** *Be sure that all hotel personnel—including the catering director, front desk manager, and general manager—are informed in writing as to what expenses the charity will cover.*

If there are musicians involved, know what instruments the group will have to provide and how many hours of rehearsal the charity must pay for. The rider should clearly state that the entertainer is responsible for paying for any rehearsal overtime beyond what's been agreed to.

These contracts can be mind-boggling to those unaccustomed to dealing with them. It's easy to miss something critical. That's why it's worth spending the money to have an attorney review the agreement. Another option is to ask a local concert promoter to be on the planning committee to provide free advice on such matters.

After lining up the star, reduce costs by getting things donated. Some hotels will provide free accommodations, and sometimes airlines will cover tickets. (Make sure these tickets are cancelable or can be changed, because they may need to be.) Sponsors love to have their pictures taken with celebrities. If possible, get the star's photo taken at the host hotel or with personnel from the airline sponsor.

A travel agent can be a great committee person and can assist in obtaining tickets and with complicated travel arrangements for celebrities and their entourages.

ROYAL TREATMENT

When dealing with a celebrity, make sure all exchanges are professional. Bend over backwards to establish a good rapport. That improves the chances of getting him or her to return in future years. Celebrities who are treated well may even lend their names to future mail campaigns and public service announcements. (Groups that want them to do this should discuss this in advance with their publicists.)

Remember that celebrities have lives of their own, too. Don't assume that someone who has agreed to appear in a show will also attend a cocktail party or go to someone's house for dinner with a charity representative and friends. Ask beforehand and include it in the contract. Some celebrities charge a fee for this. If the celebrity is unable to attend an additional function, ask if the star will autograph some items that can be auctioned off or used as raffle prizes.

And then there's the issue of jewelry, which some celebrities insist upon. In many cases, local jewelers interested in the exposure will lend a particularly showy piece for the star to wear for the event. Some of the larger watchmakers, such as Tourneau and Piaget, and some jewelers might agree to donate a watch or piece of jewelry for an upscale charity event. Offer that as an in-kind honorarium for the celebrity's appearance.

But be very careful that everyone understands the terms.

Every last detail should be in writing, as this case reported by *New York Magazine* illustrates: Former *Dynasty* star Joan Collins was to appear at a Christian Dior party for a new men's fragrance. Event planners had promised her some free designer items. But a few hours before the event, Collins' assistant called the Dior people to say the star would not be attending because she'd been disappointed with the $350 saddle bag that contained beauty products valued at about $600. When the magazine contacted Collins' assistant, she said the star had expected to be able to pick out the items herself and that she couldn't spare the time to attend.

Catastrophe nearly struck The Association of Fund Raising Professionals' 2006 conference at which Colin Powell was billed as one of its keynote speakers. At the last minute, he was unable to attend because he had to go to Supreme Court Justice Thurgood Marshall's funeral. Because it was a four-day event, the group was able to reschedule Powell for the following day.

Keep in mind that some stars don't mean to be difficult, and their refusal to do something may stem from previous bad experiences. Comedienne Joan Rivers, who stands a mere five feet tall, is always mobbed by her fans. When she appeared on stage in Miami after attending a crowded fundraising reception, she joked, "For those of you who haven't touched me yet, I'll be back down there in a few minutes."

CHAPTER 10

The Media and the Message

The theme, date, and location are set. Now it's time to start selling. Among the most effective and least costly methods of promotion: word of mouth. Ask volunteers to tell friends and colleagues and ask them to ask their friends and colleagues. Get volunteers to compile a target list that reflects a cross-section of the community's movers, shakers, and social butterflies. The most effective disseminators of information are people whose jobs put them in contact with lots of other people, such as merchants, hair stylists, accountants, lawyers, stockbrokers, physicians, and real estate agents.

MEDIA PROMOTION

Before spending money on advertising, try a method that's essentially free. Contact the largest local newspaper, or a TV or radio station (one that's popular with the people you hope to attract) and propose teaming up for a contest. Line up all three, if possible, but make sure that none of them requires exclusivity before making multiple deals. In exchange for a specific number of on-air spots or print ads promoting the event, the charity gives away a certain number of tickets each week. This creates repeated, large-scale exposure for the event and helps spur outside sales.

> **TIP** *A recent trend is for a newspaper and a television station in the same city to team up on specific projects and promotions on the premise that each will provide exposure for the other. This practice is known as "convergence." If there is such an arrangement in the city, approach one or the other participant and ask if the contest can be part of that combined effort.*

Another option is to buy advertising, just as any company does. Newspapers, magazines, and radio and television stations sometimes offer special rates for nonprofit organizations. Look for Web sites that get a lot of local traffic and approach them, too. Don't forget weekly papers. Many are distributed free, affording substantial exposure with considerably lower ad rates.

If the organization has a large corporate sponsor, ask if it could buy commercial time or ad space for the charity that would also promote the company's products or services.

> **TIP** *Ask companies that send out regular mailings or bills—banks, utilities, department stores—to allow the group to include a statement stuffer. Don't forget in-house corporate newsletters. The organization provides the actual enclosures or a camera-ready copy according to the company's specifications.*

This is a good way to get broad publicity at little cost.

INVITATION EVENTS

Follow standard direct-mail procedures when sending out invitations. Mail the invitations early and, when possible, use first-class "address correction requested" to clean up the mailing list. If mailing in bulk, follow post office procedure for separating by ZIP code.

> **TIP** *Work on increasing mailing lists well in advance of the event. Ask group members to supply a list of 10 friends who aren't already involved with the organization, along with their addresses, phone numbers, and e-mail addresses.*

That will help the group estimate how many save-the-date cards and invitations to order. Ask volunteers to help out by sending e-mail save-the-date messages, weekly news updates, and reminders to purchase tickets.

The master list should also include names and contact details for anyone who has previously contributed to the cause. If possible, acquire or exchange lists with other charities and organizations. Don't hesitate to ask committee members who are attorneys, accountants, or other professionals for lists of their clients. Merge all of these to ensure that no one gets multiple invitations. If possible, code the source of the new names as well. Check for duplicate mailings before affixing postage.

IDENTIFICATION

If the group has an identifiable image, use it. For many years, the University of Miami's Burn Center used Snuffy, a Dalmatian mascot that often appeared with a talking fire truck in the burn center's educational program (see Exhibit 10.1). Fire fighting and Dalmatians are a natural combination. The burn center used Snuffy's image for several events, dressing him appropriately for each one: For a beach party, he wore a Hawaiian shirt and sunglasses; for a scavenger hunt, he donned a Sherlock Holmes cape and pipe; for an auction, he wore a spiffy red bow tie and tuxedo. The lettering on the burn center's logo was fire-engine red, and was accompanied by the Dalmatian. Thus, people came to associate the image and colors with the charity.

Besides a distinctive symbol, invitations should be eye-catching and well designed, and include:

- The name of the event
- The sponsoring organization
- The date and time
- The location
- The purpose and theme
- Committee and chairpeople
- Cost and to whom checks should be made out
- Deadlines for response
- Honorees, if any

- What will be served (lunch, cocktails, etc.)
- Attire (formal or informal, other specifics as necessary)
- Board of directors (optional)
- Return envelope and reply card

EXHIBIT 10.1   SNUFFY THE DALMATIAN, A HIGH-PROFILE MASCOT

UM/JM Burn Center Auction

TIP *Arrange to have returns mailed to a prominent person in the community. The response generally is better if replies go to someone well-known instead of a faceless organization.*

Multipart Invitations

Mailing out an invitation gives the group more than one way to raise money. Besides the actual invitations, with the who, what, when, where, and why on them, entice people to the event with an auction, including a list of some of the top items to go on the block that night. Another option: raffle tickets. Include a raffle booklet with tear-off stubs with the invitations, making it easy for people to contribute even if they can't attend. A variation on the theme is to include one raffle ticket priced at about $25 and a book of five tickets for $100.

There is, of course, the requisite reply card. Dispense with this tired old option: "I cannot attend, but enclosed please find a donation of $_____ to support the organization's many worthy programs."

Instead, try this one: "I cannot attend, but am enclosing $100 to purchase the enclosed book of raffle tickets to support the organization, making me eligible to win a weekend in _____."

The second approach is much more likely to reap contributions.

Whenever there are additional items in the invitation, remember to add money to the budget for the extra postage. The expense will likely pay for itself because it gives potential contributors convenient options.

Advance Notice

Don't forget to have "Save-the-Date" cards printed. These should be sent out at least six weeks before the invitations, which should go out four to six weeks prior to the event.

Besides sending out individual announcements, try a broader reach as well. Travel bureaus and chambers of commerce often publish newsletters. Most daily newspapers have a community events calendar in which the event can be listed free of charge.

Make full use of e-mail. Send reminders via e-mail. (Do this judiciously so as not to add to recipients' e-mail avalanche.) Ask members to forward notices on to their clients, customers, and friends on their e-mail lists. Feature the event prominently on the organization's Web site.

Farm Aid, which singer Willie Nelson began in 1985 as a relief fund for American farmers, has become a major force in changing the way people farm, promoting organic growing techniques and educating the public about the importance of wholesome food made available by U.S. farmers. Among the ways Farm Aid spreads its message and builds donor support is through an e-mail newsletter, one of the reasons the charity's Web-based donations increased from $20,000 in 2003 to $200,000 in 2005.

> **TIP** *Ask members who have Web sites to provide a link to the organization's site or information about the event.*

If the group has the budget to do so and a large enough event to justify it, buy time on the Internet through one of the providers (AOL, MSN, COMCAST, etc.). If the event includes a celebrity appearance, buy three hours on the Internet to have the celebrity appear in a cyberspace chat room, talking with real people and helping to promote the cause. Popular blogs can also be used to add some excitement or even controversy to an upcoming event. If people are talking about the event they are more likely to attend.

A FRESH LOOK

It's hard to imagine that there can be anything new and different when it comes to invitations. Yet, some creative types continue to delight and surprise. Make a collection of creative invitations that come to group members from other organizations. They may help spark some ideas when the time comes.

Another way to draw attention is to send out small stuffed animals with notes of invitation attached to their collars. These little critters are eye-catching and are sometimes less expensive than standard invitations. Or appeal to the media through its collective stomach. Attach the invitation to a box of gourmet cookies or chocolates.

Ordering Invitations

First, figure out how many invitations are needed (cover the mailing list then add 25 percent for publicity extras and a back-up supply). Next, determine how many pieces will be in the invitation (outside envelope, inside envelope, invitation, reply card, return envelope, personal note card, raffle tickets, auction sampler, etc.).

Hire a graphic artist to design an appealing invitation unless someone within the group is creative and well-versed in producing professional-looking invitations. Make sure the artist understands postal regulations regarding the size and weight of the invitations. Discuss how many colors of ink and the kinds of paper that will be used. Discuss the design: How expensive should it look? It shouldn't appear as lavish as what might be sent for a high-end wedding or corporate event, or it might appear the group has spent too much money. The exception to this rule is when the cost of the invitations is totally underwritten and this is clearly stated on the invitation.

The most cost-effective way to produce invitations is to do it in-house on a computer. Office supply stores sell all sorts of software and paper that allow amateurs to produce stylish invitations with matching envelopes at a fraction of the price of those created by a professional printer. They also take considerably less time to make, which can be a lifesaver if all the program details aren't nailed down until just a few weeks before the event.

If someone offers to underwrite the invitations, it's still better to produce them on the computer and put the rest of the money toward postage and other event expenses. For those who absolutely must have professionally printed invitations, ask around for reputable printers, get at least three bids, and check references, making sure the quality and timeliness of the jobs were acceptable. Request that envelopes be provided in advance so volunteers can begin addressing them while the invitations and other materials are being printed. Printers often have equipment to fold and collate invitations. Ask for it. It's a great time-saver.

No matter who creates the invitation, always have at least three people read the invitation proof before producing hundreds of copies. Double-check the date, time, place, and the spelling of committee members' and sponsors' names. Make sure no names have been left out. Find someone not involved in the project to look it over, too. This only sounds silly until the time the group sends out hundreds of invitations that lack a time or date, or contain erroneous information. While misspellings may seem minor, they can cause hard feelings and might cost the charity a valuable volunteer or contribution. Justified or not, it may also reflect upon the overall caliber of the charity. Finally, the executive director should scrutinize a proof of the invitation and sign off on it.

Time Frame

Invitation planning and production must be done well in advance. Invitations should be mailed four to six weeks before a major event. Add a minimum of two weeks to have the invitations designed and a week to print them (if doing them in-house) or as much as a month to have a professional printer make them. Give the committee two weeks to address and mail the invitations. That means the process should start at least three months before the event. Add an extra month if possible to allow for missed deadlines and other unexpected delays.

Getting Them Out

Set up a schedule for addressing invitations. Keep a master mailing list on a widely accessible computer (as well as a backup file that gets backed up every day or two). Print out a copy from which volunteers can work.

Maintain control of the mailing by having volunteers do it at central location. As each invitation is addressed, have someone check off the name on the master list. (Don't forget to transfer it to the computerized file. If people can't gather at a central location to address the envelopes—many prefer working at home—ask that they return the completed invitations to the office so they can all be mailed together.

Committee members should add personal notes to the invitations going to their personal friends. These are inserted with the invitation. It's possible to mail invitations at bulk rate for two hundred pieces or more, but it requires advance planning and a permit and the invitations must be sorted into boxes according to ZIP code. For the most up-to-date details on fees and requirements, go to the U.S. Post Office's comprehensive Web site (www.usps.com).

Once the invitations are addressed, the person in charge should personally take them to the post office. It's a good way to ensure they really are in the mail and not sitting on someone's kitchen table.

FOLLOWING UP

The next step requires working the phones. Using the same master list, assign portions to each committee member. All mailing lists should have phone numbers on them for just this sort of follow-up.

> **TIP** *Following up the invitations with phone calls significantly boosts attendance.*

It's generally best to provide callers with a script that includes a key reason for someone to attend: "I'm Jane Doherty, a volunteer with the XYZ Charity. Mrs. Smith asked me to follow up on the invitation she sent you to our event. She was sure that you would like to join her that evening. May I put you down for two seats?"

For a corporation, try something like, "I know your corporation will want to join our other corporate sponsors, which include the ABC and DEF corporations."

Typically, people wait until the last minute to decide whether or not to attend an event. Keep after them. Make a second round of calls, if necessary. Have some volunteers call business people at their offices during the day. Have others call people at home in the evening. If possible, have someone send a short e-mail or personal note as a reminder.

PROMOTION

While all of the above is going on, the group should be getting the word out to the public. Along with ticket sales, this is one of the most important aspects of producing an event.

It is imperative that one very responsible person take charge of this. If the group does not have an experienced volunteer who can handle it, consider hiring a publicist or a public relations firm, if the group can afford it. The additional promotion and media coverage a professional may be able to arrange generally equates to far more than the fee that person will charge.

Another option: If there's a college or university in town that offers a public relations or marketing program, contact the department head and find out if one of the top seniors might be interested in working to promote the event as an internship for college credit or a small stipend.

MINDING THE MEDIA

The most effective means of getting the word out is via the news media. Prepare a detailed media contact list. Include all radio and television stations, newspapers (weeklies, college, school, in-house newsletters), and local magazines. Check with the local chamber of commerce and scour the Yellow Pages to make sure the list is comprehensive. Most newspapers and TV stations have Web sites on which are listed the appropriate contacts and details on how to reach them. Call to inquire about deadlines and verify that the information on the Web site is current. Get a fax number, too.

PUBLIC SERVICE ANNOUNCEMENTS

Prepare a concise news release and direct it to the person who handles public service announcements (PSAs) at each area radio and television station. These are 15-, 30-, or 60-second spots donated by the station and usually read by an announcer. These must be short and to the point. Just give the basics (who, what, when, where, and why, plus a contact).

Keep in mind that the group's PSA will compete against many others for air time, so the more creative it is, the more likely it is to be noticed. One way to draw attention is to have celebrities tape the messages. If someone in the group knows a celebrity who will be appearing in town, call in advance to see if the star would be willing to tape a PSA to help support the cause and event. Arrange this through the celebrity's personal manager or publicist.

For radio and television promotion, arrange for the PSA three to four weeks before the event. If possible, have a large company sponsor the cost of producing the PSA or buying air time for the message to be broadcast. In exchange, give the sponsor credit in the message.

Sometimes it's possible to tie into public service themes run by the radio or television stations. Some stations sponsor year-long promotions, focusing on such things as children's issues, health concerns, or anti-drug campaigns. If the group fits into that category, contact the station to see if it will include the group's message with the campaign.

> **TIP** *Public Service Announcements (known as PSAs) used in combination with ticket giveaways encourage radio and televisions stations to get involved.*

TALK, TALK

Radio talk shows can help promote the event, too. Having someone from the group appear on the show, either in an interview, taking calls from the public, or both, can provide great exposure. Shoot for the morning or evening "drive-time" shows, which generally get the largest audiences because people are headed to or from work and have the radio on. Find an interesting highlight or angle related to the event and select the best spokesperson to appear on the show to discuss the event and what will happen there. The person should talk about what the money raised will do for people in the community. Radio stations can help promote the event with event-related contests (paid for by sponsors).

PRINT MEDIA

Newspapers have community calendars, weekend entertainment guides, and sections geared to specific segments of the community. Use them all. These are usually well read and can draw a great deal of attention to the event in a small space—and with no outlay of money. Buy the paper for a few days and search out the departments, columns, or sections for which the event is suitable. Look for charitable causes, entertainment, features, monthly arts and events calendars, sports or education listings if they are applicable, local briefs, and any other appropriate notices.

Send releases to daily newspapers four to six weeks in advance of the event. And don't assume various departments in a newspaper swap releases. Each gets hundreds a day. Send one to each department. Also, send a news release to every appropriate editor. Use a cover letter. And, on the chance the paper will want to cover the event itself, send a fax reminder two or three days in advance and call the day before the event.

For monthly magazines, the lead time for releases usually is eight to ten weeks, although it can be more than that. For convention calendars, send information as soon as it's available, because these are often printed far in advance (quarterly or semi-annually).

MAKING NEWS

In addition to PSAs, there is news coverage. Start by distributing press kits. They should each contain copies of the group's:

- Cover letter
- News release
- Fact sheet
- Organization information
- Sponsor list
- Poster (if applicable)
- Photos. Most newspapers prefer these in CD form or sent via e-mail.

No matter how important group members think their event is, much of the news media won't think it's newsworthy. There are hundreds of good causes seeking coverage constantly. Generally, the trick is to find an angle that will interest an editor. Be creative. Remember that what news media look for is the "news peg": not a simple advance on the event, but some current trend or happening that might make it newsworthy. Be sure to convey what the fundraising will mean to real people, preferably those in the local community.

PROMOTION TIME FRAME

Four to six weeks before the event, send out the news release, mentioning the story angle briefly. Follow it up with a call to the appropriate editor. If it's possible to reach the right person, quickly and succinctly explain the event and the story idea.

> **TIP** *If there's a celebrity scheduled to appear, the star may be willing to do phone interviews with local media. Don't be afraid to ask.*

Make sure the person whose name is being given to the paper has agreed to be interviewed and photographed for publication. Then supply the editor with the name, phone, and e-mail of that person. Follow up a few days later to make sure that the reporter was able to make contact with the person recommended.

Other Publicity

Take advantage of anyplace willing to post a poster or flyer. Don't forget such spots as billboards, the backs of grocery store receipts, on grocery sacks and milk cartons, motel marquees, pamphlets in convenience stores, libraries, store bulletin boards, visitor centers, and table displays in restaurants. Some merchants will allow charities to place posters in their windows. Check with television cable companies that air community news listings or closed-circuit systems at local hotels. Check with movie theaters, which sometimes run announcements for charities before the film starts. In many cities, there are Web sites dedicated to charitable and other local events. Ask a computer-savvy member to research this.

Publicity Stunts

Use these judiciously. They should be offbeat, but not crazy or offensive. Using local personalities (radio disk jockeys, news anchors, etc.) can generate advance publicity. For example, for a chili cookoff, hand out free chili samples at supermarkets the week before the event. The weathercasters at many local TV stations are available to help promote charitable events.

Pre-Events

Think of pre-events as appetizers before the main course. They aren't always necessary but they can whet the public's appetite for the event.

Relatively simple pre-events include having an author sign books at the local bookstore or recording artists appear at a music store. If the event will include a guest chef, try to arrange for that person to conduct a cooking demonstration at a local kitchen or department store. Such pre-events draw people interested in that star to the preview, at which it may be possible to sell tickets for the main event.

CHAPTER 11

The Final Countdown

Somehow the team members have maneuvered their way through the obstacle course of tasks and personalities that converge during the planning of an event. The raison d'etre is almost at hand.

For that rare breed gifted with extreme organizational skills, there's little left to do. Everyone else will likely work right up to the wire.

But there comes a point at which everyone must concede that everything is done that can reasonably be done and that's it. Do not stay up the entire night prior to the event before coming to this realization. A good night's sleep is among the most important tasks on the list for anyone who hopes to think clearly and have sufficient energy and patience for the big day.

CHECKING IT TWICE

Those who have faithfully followed the instructions in the previous chapters will have a nice, fat loose-leaf notebook as well as a complete electronic file (with at least one backup copy, of course) to make sure everything has been covered. Now is the time to recheck. Go through the list of assignments to double-check that each task has been completed.

The day before the event:

- Remind support staff to be at the site at a specific time (well before the event's starting time) the next day.

- Check with all the vendors to make sure they know what time they must arrive. Get the phone numbers at which they can be contacted outside of business hours.

169

- Check with all committee chairpeople to check how to reach them if they won't be at their usual numbers. Make sure the chairpeople have spoken with everyone on their lists: the decorator, band, caterer, florist, etc. If there isn't one already, compile a one-page directory of the key people who might be needed along with their home and cell phone numbers.

- Ensure that anyone who needs a script for the evening (which the event manager and staff crafted so that everyone would know what was to happen and when) has one and understands his or her part.

> **TIP** *Enlist a few people (family members, trusted friends, or assistants) to lend a hand on the day of the event to deal with unexpected problems. Dispatch them to put out the smaller fires while staff members handle the larger tasks.*

LAST-MINUTE NEEDS

No matter what the event, there are items people almost always need at the last minute but won't have unless someone has planned ahead and assembled them. Pack everything up in advance. Here is what to take along:

Administrative

- Contact list with home, work and cell phone numbers
- Loose-leaf notebook with all contracts, contacts, etc. (plus extra paper with holes already punched in)
- Payment for entertainer

Audiovisual

- Laptop computer and backup disks
- Black electrical tape/silver reflective tape
- Audio and video cassettes
- Extension cords—industrial strength and length
- Three-prong converters

- Flashlights
- Needle and thread
- Safety pins
- Cell phones/chargers

Paper Products, Office Supplies, and Related Items

- Toilet tissue
- Facial tissue
- Paper towels
- Soap
- Trash bags
- Paper
- Scissors
- Signs
- Staple gun
- Masking and transparent tape
- Felt-tip waterproof markers (various sizes and colors)
- Paper clips
- Self-stick labels (various sizes)
- Poster board
- Pens

First-Aid Kit

- Adhesive tape
- Bandages
- Stretch and gauze bandages
- Scissors/knife
- Tweezers
- Aspirin
- Antacid
- Alcohol and/or peroxide for disinfectant

- Sunscreen
- Insect repellent

Staff Food

- Coffee
- Cold drinks
- Ice/ice chest
- Munchies

Pack up everything the day before, including the outfit for the event. Then, on the day itself, the box or suitcase is ready, making departure easier.

If the event is in a hotel, arrange to check in a day or two in advance to unpack, get familiar with the place, and inform everyone how to make contact. Let the front desk staff know that calls might be coming in and keep them abreast of how to reach a key person, including that person's cell phone number. With all those things attended to, get a good night's sleep.

REGISTRATION

Registration sets the tone for the event because it is the first impression the group makes on those attending. If they have to wait in long lines, or if they're treated rudely or encounter problems, guests may be turned off before they get in the door. To avoid this, place the most personable and intelligent people on registration duty. Make sure they know that their primary job is signing in those attending, ascertaining that guests have paid and directing them where to go next.

Usually, the registration process is set up about three hours before the event. Even if the ballroom is not ready, registration tables should be. They should be the first things that are functioning, since they are the guests' first stop.

There should be enough eight-foot-long tables to allow people to spread out a bit. Use long tables, covered attractively, with highly visible signs posted above them. It may require using several tables, dividing them alphabetically, with each table handling a third or a fourth of the alphabet. Reserve another table for troubleshooting, and one for VIPs.

Supply three or four chairs behind each table for registration staff, even though they will probably wind up standing as guests file in.

> **TIP** *Don't put signs on the tables themselves, because they will be covered up as people gather. Hang them from above.*

Make sure additional signs clearly point the way from the parking lot to the tables. Make sure there are enough lights and electrical outlets.

It is always better to have too many registration workers than too few. For a gathering of 100 people, only one registration worker may be needed per table. For 500 people, it's apt to take four workers per table.

If registration workers have to eat, serve food early so they have a chance to get dressed. Make sure everyone on the registration staff knows how to dress for the event. They typically wear the same type of apparel as those who will attend. When using computers, make sure they are all hooked up, functioning, and in a secure area.

For large-scale events (such as tournaments, a-thons, or fairs): Set up a separate set of registration tables for supervisors, referees, athletes, vendors, and sponsors. It makes sense to separate their check-in from that of the spectators, because they have different needs, may arrive at different times, and will need their own registration forms, gifts, and information packets.

For an event with fixed seating: Give everyone something with the number of their seat on it. It should be a slip of paper big enough not to be easily misplaced, but small enough to fit in a jacket pocket or small purse.

To prevent party crashers: Distribute stickers, pins, or disposable bracelets to guests to identify them.

If registration desk must collect money: Make sure the workers are equipped to do this. They should have a secure place to keep the money as well as calculators and lists of those who have not paid. When taking credit cards at the registration tables (highly recommended), have a phone connected to the credit-card companies for immediate authorization.

Registration should never take more than an hour. If there are sufficient volunteers, each armed with a guest list, it's not hard to do. All registration staff should be supplied with a list of everyone who is attending, listed both alphabetically and by table so that people need not wait in line for more than a few minutes.

> **TIP** *Besides having sufficient staff at the registration desk, have additional greeters near the registration tables and in the main room to guide people to the proper spots.*

Anticipating problems: No matter how good a job the committee does in arranging seating, there should be a troubleshooter to handle last-minute changes that inevitably crop up. When this happens, a registration worker should immediately direct the person to the troubleshooter, who will make sure the problem is resolved. This way, everyone isn't delayed.

As with other aspects of the event, try to anticipate problems that might arise. When using computers, have printed backup lists in case the computers conk out. If there is a problem with a guest's registration, be sure workers are pleasant at all times. They should apologize to guests for the problem and escort them to the troubleshooter's table, where someone will work with them until the problem is resolved.

> **TIP** *Assigned seating isn't always necessary or desirable. At an auction or informal affair, let guests seat themselves. Registration for open seating takes much less time.*

If the event is lengthy, try to arrange shifts for registration workers. Don't leave someone on duty for more than an hour or two at a time, because registration is a tiring job. Try to reward registration workers by giving them a good table at the event. Provide their meal free (if the charity can afford to or at a reduced charge), and make sure they get to see the show without charge.

CHAPTER 12

After Words

For better or for worse, it's over now. However the event turned out it will surely provide valuable lessons for future efforts. That's why it's important to conduct a thorough review and critique one to three weeks after the event.

Once everyone has recharged and gotten a little distance from the event, the chairperson or a responsible volunteer should gather top committee people, staff, and key volunteers, to celebrate its conclusion. Explain to those invited that the group is holding a luncheon (or breakfast or coffee and dessert) to review the event. The gathering can take place either in a restaurant meeting room or at someone's home. A meal or refreshments of some sort will help boost attendance.

The charity should not foot the bill for this. Either the chairperson should pay or find someone willing to underwrite the expense.

If the gathering takes place at a restaurant, try scheduling it for a time when it's not busy so it won't burden the wait staff or kitchen. The best option is a restaurant at which a lead member of the group dines frequently and knows the manager or owner. Let that person know that the group includes influential people who dine out regularly. Point out what great exposure it would be for the restaurant in exchange for meeting space and a light meal (provided at no charge, of course).

> **TIP** *Whether the chairperson or someone else pays for the meal or space, make sure to tip the servers well.*

Start the meeting by thanking everyone for their hard work. Hand out the evaluation forms at the start of the gathering or send them via e-mail or snail mail a few days in advance so everyone has time to review them. Make sure the sheets have plenty of room in which people can write their thoughts and comments.

Go through each item and seek input on ways to make the next event better. Use the post-event evaluation form contained in this chapter as the guide for the critique. Tailor the form to accommodate the specifics of the event. Make sure there are enough copies so everyone who attends has one and there are some left over.

Someone should lead the discussion, perhaps a popular volunteer, the special event coordinator, or executive director. Keep the mood casual and friendly. Stress that the goal is to make the next event even better, not to assign blame. Allow constructive criticism only.

Finally, ask each person to talk about a highlight or to share feedback they received from a guest who attended the event. The person taking notes should compile these comments on the post-event evaluation master sheet. Put the date of the event at the top of the summary evaluation form and the date of the meeting. Place one completed post-event evaluation summary in the event file or event notebook as well. It will come in handy next time.

After the meeting, use the summary to create a computer document that can be e-mailed or sent by mail, with a cover note, including an additional thank you to each volunteer and staff member.

> **TIP** *Another nice touch is to send each volunteer a small gift, such as a framed invitation from the event, monogrammed stationery, or a small crystal box.*

POST-EVENT EVALUATION

Event

- Did the group conduct an informal survey to determine the appeal to potential attendees?
- Did the date set afford adequate time to properly organize and promote the event?

- Did the charity attract the audience it was after? If not, why?
- Did the charity establish a goal for net amount raised? Was the goal attained?
- Did it attract new people who might become donors?
- Did guests enjoy themselves? Would they attend again?
- What changes might help improve that?
- Did it occur at the same time as another large event?
- Would holding it at a different time or on a different day matter?
- How many people attended? Enough to make it worth doing?
- Is it likely to grow over the years?
- Did the event need a rain date?
- Was it held at the optimum time of year?

Committees

- Was there written criteria for selecting committee chairpeople?
- Did each committee member have a written assignment or goals for the group?
- Did committees meet regularly enough? Too often?
- Did they complete assignments on time and within budget?
- Did the chairperson stay in frequent contact with the event manager?
- Did the chairperson ask for assistance or advice when needed?
- Were there enough/too many people on each committee?
- Have any new leaders emerged from within the committees?
- Did each chairperson have a co-chairperson who could head up the next event?

Location

- How well did the site suit the event?
- Was it a good fit for the number of people organizers anticipated would attend?
- Would a larger or smaller venue work better the next time?
- Did weather play a factor?
- Did the group buy weather insurance?

- Who provided and paid for liability insurance?
- Was there enough equipment (seats, tables, kitchen gear)?
- Could the event have taken place in a less expensive site or a less costly form?
- Was the venue convenient for those attending? Easy to find?
- Were all spaces used during the event accessible to people with physical challenges?
- Was public transportation available nearby?
- Was parking adequate and reasonably priced?
- Were any permits required?
- Did the group obtain and/or pay for security personnel?

Budget

- Were there best-case and worse-case budgets?
- Did organizers carefully calculate expenses prior to setting a per-person cost to attend?
- Did the group stay within the budget guidelines?
- How much did the event cost?
- How much did it net after expenses? (Include a separate estimated cost for staff time.)
- Did any budget items significantly exceed estimates?
- Was the amount spent consistent with the group's goals and image?
- Did the group raise enough money, after paying expenses, to consider holding another event like it?
- Was there enough money in advance? Adequate cash flow?
- Was bookkeeping kept current throughout the event development in order to track expenses?
- Did the accounting system adequately track all income and expenses?
- Were all bills paid in a timely manner?
- Were all contracts negotiated with an eye to maximizing profit?
- What items were missing from the budget?
- If the group did it again, how might costs be reduced?

- Was there a list of specific items or costs for which to seek underwriting?
- Were there any corporate or personal sponsors?
- What might be added?
- Were there any financial surprises?

Promotion

- Was there a written plan for promoting the event? Was the plan reviewed by staff, volunteers, and/or a public relations consultant?
- Was there a written timeline with staff assignments to obtain adequate publicity?
- Did news releases get to the appropriate people?
- Was the media list correct, including the contact people, their titles, e-mail and office addresses?
- How might the group attract more publicity?
- Was there a preview event?
- If a staff member handled event promotion, did that person need more help?
- If volunteers took care of publicity, might they have benefited from professional help?
- Did the group stay within the promotions budget?
- Were mailings and e-mails sent out in a timely manner?
- Did the event make it into all the community calendars available?
- How well did the charity make use of local media, including cable access stations?
- How well did the group use e-mail and the Internet?
- Was there enough coordination and follow-up?
- Did committee members write personal notes that were sent with invitations, to friends and business associates, to encourage their attendance? Did they make personal follow-up calls?
- Were flyers, posters, and invitations attractive and did they contain easily readable information?

- Were they properly distributed, mailed, and posted?
- Were mailing lists up to date? Were a lot of invitations returned?

Registration

- Could guests find the registration table easily?
- Were there enough people on duty to prevent long waits?
- Was there adequate staff at the registration table to handle problems?
- Were there any complaints from guests?
- Were volunteers adequately trained?
- Did the group have all the computer skills needed?
- Was the registration staff properly dressed and courteous?
- Were guest(s) registered alphabetically by last name?
- Was there a list of guests by table assigned?
- Did the group use commercially available special event software? If so, what kind?
- Were computers situated so they did not need special outlets or connections?
- How well did the computers function?

Food

- Who selected the menu? Was it within budget?
- Did anyone in the group hold a thorough tasting before the event?
- Any comments about the food or service?
- How was the presentation?
- If group members cooked or brought food, were there any problems?
- Were there enough people setting up and cleaning up?
- Would it have cost less at another location or if the group had hired a different company?
- How did the group accommodate special dietary restrictions?
- How was the beverage and liquor service? Does anything there need tweaking?

- Was the group able to get food, liquor, bottled water, and drinks donated or underwritten?
- Did anyone attempt to get food and/or liquor donated through vendor sponsorship?

Entertainment

- Did the charity make the most of the promotional potential of high-profile entertainers?
- Did the charity hire a talent service to get the best price for the talent hired?
- Were contracts adequately negotiated and reviewed?
- Did an attorney review contracts for extra costs and liability?
- Was good or better entertainment available for the same price or less?
- Did the contract for the celebrity include making a public service announcement for the organization?
- Did the group obtain sponsorship for the celebrity's transportation, lodging, and related costs?
- Could this event have succeeded without entertainment/celebrity participation?
- Did the entertainment add to the event? Was it age appropriate for the audience?
- Did it fit the theme?
- Did it stay within budget?
- Was it worth the expense?
- Did people dance (if there was a DJ or band) and/or enjoy the show?
- Were there any problems with sound or lighting?

Event Management

- What were the criteria used to decide if the event was to be managed by a staff member or consultant?
- Did the manager make all assignments clear and in written form?

- Was there a written timeline for producing the event, including staff assignments?
- Was there regular follow-up with committee chairpeople on their committees' progress?
- Did the manager handle contract negotiations? Make efforts to cut costs where possible?
- Did the manager have sufficient staff available?
- How did the manager relate to paid staff and volunteers?
- Was the manager accessible when problems came up?
- Did the manager handle all aspects of the event professionally?
- Were there any personality clashes, logistical errors, or emergencies worth noting?

CHAPTER 13

Tools of the Trade

There are scores of expert sources and resources even small organizations can call upon for advice and inspiration. Following is a sampling of them. Countless more can be found via the Internet. (**Please note that due to the rapidly changing online world, this information may become incorrect over time. It is meant to be a starting point.)

AUCTIONS/RAFFLES

American Fundraising Auctions

953 N. Lake Adair Blvd.
Orlando, FL 32804
Phone: (877) 896-4500
Fax: 407-872-7042
www.americanfundraisingauctions.com

Conducts turnkey live auctions nationally, raising more than $2 million yearly for clients. It provides everything for the event, including international vacations and jewelry.

Auction Anything.com

425 S. Chickasaw Trail, #16B
Orlando, FL 32825
Phone: (800) 866-8009
Fax: (407) 540-9574
www.auctionanything.com

Supplies charities with online auction capabilities.

Auctionpay

13221 S.W. 68th Pkwy., Suite 460
Portland, OR 97223
Phone: (800) 276-5992
Fax: (503) 597-0379
www.auctionpay.com

Provides comprehensive fundraising tools, including event software, customized online registration and donation, and secure, convenient payment processing.

AuctionStar/Silent Auction Software

4211 Villanova St.
Houston, TX 77005
Phone: (713) 665-1231
Fax: (713) 667-8325
www.barcodedauctions.com

CrestWare Inc. provides AuctionStar® software and services for silent auction fundraising. It tracks donor, item, and guest information; produces the auction catalog and event materials; handles event invoicing and credit-card processing; and provides purchase statistics and other features.

cMarket Inc.

1 Main St, 10th Floor
Cambridge, MA 02142

Phone: (866) 621-0330
Fax: (617) 374-9015
www.cmarket.com

Helps fundraisers build and protect their donor bases, attract sponsors, and improve fundraising results via online auctions.

The Gavel Group

13805 Alton Pkwy., Suite B
Irvine, CA 92618
Phone: (949) 900-2020
Fax: (949) 900-2021
www.gavelgroup.com

Supplies no-risk auction items to nonprofits for use in fundraising. Items include travel (high-end and family oriented) and retail items. It also provides auctioneering and auction production services.

Missionfish

www.missionfish.org

Helps individual support their favorite causes through trading on eBay. Provides technology, tools, and support to thousands of organizations and donors, the exclusive charity solution provider for eBay Giving Works, and a service of the Points of Light Foundation, which enables charities to establish their own online eBay stores.

Rafflepartner.org

5711 Industry Lane, Unit 31
Frederick, MD 21704
Phone: (240) 529-1022
Fax: (240) 529-1029
www.rafflepartner.org

Helps nonprofit organizations raise funds over the Internet. Ideal for schools, charities, churches, community groups, and sports teams.

Steiner Sports Memorabilia

33 Le Count Place
New Rochelle, NY 10801
Phone: (914) 307–1021
Fax: (914) 632–1102
www.steinersports.com

Handles authentic, hand-signed collectibles, autographed memorabilia by athletes such as Derek Jeter, Joe Namath, Larry Bird, and Muhammad Ali for fundraising auctions.

CELEBRITY SOURCES

American Federation of Television and Radio Artists (AFTRA)

Los Angeles National Office
5757 Wilshire Boulevard, 9th Floor
Los Angeles, CA 90036
Phone: (323) 634–8203
Fax: (323) 634–8121
www.aftra.org

Or

New York National Office
260 Madison Avenue
New York, NY 10016
Phone: (212) 532–0800
Fax: (212) 686–4925
www.aftra.org

Represents people in the television and radio fields.

American Society of Composers, Authors, and Publishers (ASCAP)

1 Lincoln Plaza
New York, NY 10023
Phone: (212) 621–6000

Fax: (212) 724-9064
www.ascap.com

With a membership of more than 240,000 composers, songwriters, lyricists, and music producers, this organization licenses and protects artists' rights to their works.

Celebrity Talent International

33 Gateview Drive
Fallbrook, CA 92028
Phone: (866) 803-6739 or (760) 731-3900
Fax: (760) 731-3969
www.celebritytalent.net

With 30-plus years in the business, CTI attracts big-name performers, speakers, television and movie stars, as well as pro athletes. Helps groups find a celebrity that fits their image and budget, coordinates phone interviews, air and ground transportation, and will handle full production and technical services when needed. Provides fact sheets on topics such as corporate sponsorship.

Screen Actors Guild (SAG)

5757 Wilshire Boulevard
Los Angeles, CA 99036
Phone: (323) 954-1600

Or

360 Madison Avenue, 12th Floor
New York, NY 10017
Phone: (212) 944-1030
www.sag.org

A labor union that protects performers and supplies contact information. Those looking to contact a star can get that from the Actors to Locate service at (323) 549-6737.

SPEAKERS' BUREAUS

Greater Talent Network

437 Fifth Avenue
New York, NY 10016
Phone: (212) 645-2000 or (800) 326-4211
Fax: (212) 627-1471
www.gtnspeakers.com

Can book luminaries from many walks of life, including athletes, entrepreneurs, actors, and politicians, as speakers for events. Check the Web site for a full list of celebrities available; read the page that lists the 10 questions to ask before hiring a speakers' bureau.

The Harry Walker Agency Inc.

355 Lexington Avenue, 21st Floor
New York, NY 10017
Phone: (646) 227-4900
Fax: (646) 227-4901
www.harrywalker.com

Many of the nation's foremost VIPs, including former presidents, economists, media people, and political figures, as well as athletes and actors can be booked through this long-lived firm. The firm also offers My-HarryWalker, an easy-to-use Internet site on which clients can manage their events from anywhere.

CHARITY WATCHDOGS/DATABASES

Better Business Bureau Wise Giving Alliance

4200 Wilson Boulevard, Suite 800
Arlington, VA 22203
Phone: (703) 276-0100
Fax: (703) 525-8277
www.give.org

A nationwide clearinghouse of information on nonprofit organizations with reports on charities based on comprehensive standards for charity accountability. Offers many publications and detailed reports on charities. This organization arose from a merger in 2001 of the National Charities Information Bureau and the Council of Better Business Bureaus' Foundation. To expand its reporting, it now has an online reporting system. Charities are not charged for evaluations. Charities that meet standards can apply to participate in the Alliance's National Charity Seal Program.

Charity Navigator

1200 MacArthur Boulevard, Second Floor
Mahwah, NJ 07430
Phone: (201) 818-1288
Fax: (201) 818-4694
www.charitynavigator.org

Maintains information and ratings on 5,000 charities with analysis of their financial health. Supplies free information to the public.

GuideStar

4801 Courthouse Street
Suite 220
Williamsburg, VA 23188
Phone: (757) 229-4631
www.guidestar.org

A leading source of information on U.S. nonprofit organizations. Access information on more than 1 million nonprofit corporations at the group's Web site. Enter organization data, customize data extracts, and research grants.

CREDIT CARDS

American Express

200 Vesey Street, Mailcode: 01-34-10
New York, NY 10285
Phone: (212) 640-6625
Fax: (212) 640-0215
www.americanexpress.com/give

The worldwide travel, financial, and network services company offers the American Express Donation Site (americanexpress.com/give), which provides card members with the convenience of donating dollars or Membership Rewards® points online to some 1 million charitable organizations. Charitable organizations can promote the donation site via their own channels to raise funds online.

Mastercard International

2000 Purchase Street
Purchase, NY 10577
Phone: (914) 249-5579
Fax: (914) 249-4107
www.mastercardmerchant.com

Provides a convenient donation option.

Donor Gifts

Ameropean Corporation

7 Corporate Drive, Unit # 108
North Haven, CT 06473
Phone: (800) 466-4648
Fax: (203) 234-8820
www.leatherbookmarks.com

Supplies custom-designed leather bookmarks and accessories that can be used as recognition gifts to support fundraising programs.

Art as a Catalyst

4210 Howard Avenue
Kensington, MD 20895
Phone: (301) 493-5577
Fax: (301) 493-5578
www.artasacatalyst.org

Creates socially responsible, hand-crafted donor recognition gifts and awards to generate funds for arts enrichment, charitable, and educational programs. Purchases also create jobs for special needs groups.

Camelot Pewter Co., Inc.

12302 Patterson Avenue
Richmond, VA 23238
Phone: (804) 784-3770
Fax: (804) 784-2785
www.camelotpewter.com

Produces hand-crafted lead-free pewter. Computerized engraving allows most items to be personalized with either the charity's logo or names, dates, titles, etc. The company specializes in tasteful gifts for donor recognition, awards presentation, special events, golf and tennis tournaments, retirements, party favors, speakers, etc.

David Howell & Company

405 Adams Street
Bedford Hills, NY 10507
Phone: (914) 666-4080, ext. 13
Fax: (914) 666-2721
www.davidhowell.com

Provides high-quality custom donor gifts such as bookmarks, ornaments, letter openers, and more. All made in the United States.

Framing Success

2700 Avenger Drive, Suite 100
Virginia Beach, VA 23452
Phone: (800) 200-2044
Fax: (800) 576-3726
www.framingsuccess.com

Offers custom certificate frames featuring the organization's name and logo embossed on the matboard.

The Gavel Group

13805 Alton Parkway, Suite B
Irvine, CA 92618
www.gavelgroup.com

Provides no-risk auction items to nonprofits for use in fundraising events. Items include travel (high-end and family) and retail items, auctioneering and production services.

FUNDRAISING CONSULTANTS/EVENT MANAGEMENT

Alexander Haas Martin & Partners

Piedmont Place, 3520 Piedmont Road NE, Suite 300
Atlanta, GA 30305
Phone: (800) 490-8039
Fax: (404) 524-2992

Specializes in work with museums and cultural organizations throughout the country, offering pre-campaign counsel, development and membership, staff training.

Barton G.

BGW Design Limited Inc.
3628 NE Second Ave.
Miami, FL 33137
Phone: (305) 576-8888
Fax: (305) 576-8887

Offers event production around the world, supplying all of the event/ catering/production management necessary. Barton G. also runs a glamorous Miami restaurant (1427 West Ave., Miami, FL 33139) and a catering company.

Changing Our World, Inc.

220 East 42nd Street, 7th Floor
New York, NY 10017
Phone: (212) 499-0866
Fax: (212) 499-9075
www.changingourworld.com

A philanthropic services company that offers tailored fundraising, philanthropic services, and integrated technology solutions that combine innovation with sound fundamentals. The company's services include feasibility and planning studies, capital campaigns and major gift initiatives, development outsourcing, planned giving, online fundraising, and communications.

Expert Events

123 S. Broad Street, Suite 2035
Philadelphia, PA 19109
Phone: (215) 546-9422
Fax: (215) 546-9437
www.expertevents.com

The company specializes in long-term planning for milestone and fundraising events for nonprofits, corporations, and academic institutions. Services include strategic planning and goal setting, corporate sponsorship support, event planning and production.

Great Performances Inc.

287 Spring Street
New York, NY 10013
Phone: (212) 727-2424
Fax: (212) 727-7103
www.greatperformances.com

A New York–based catering and events company that produces events ranging from intimate soirees in private homes to international conferences with participants such as Bill Clinton and Bill Gates. Also operates eight restaurants at New York City cultural institutions.

The Oram Group

275 Madison Avenue
New York, NY 10016
Phone: (212) 889-2244
Fax: (212) 986-2731

Or

328 Duncan Street
San Francisco, CA 94131
Phone: (415) 821-2534
Fax: (415) 643-7925
www.oramgroup.com

Helps clients in the fields of education, religion, health, welfare, social action, civil rights, the environment, and visual and performing arts hone a competitive edge in the philanthropic marketplace, offering training, management, and other services to the nonprofit sector.

Raising More Money

2100 N. Pacific Street
Seattle, WA 98103
Phone: (206) 709-9400
Fax: (206) 352-9492
www.raisingmoremoney.com

Trains and coaches nonprofit organizations to implement a mission-based system for raising sustainable funding from individual donors in an effort to end the concern about holding fundraisers while still building committed lifelong donors.

RuffaloCODY

65 Kirkwood N. Road SW
Cedar Rapids, Iowa 52406
Phone: (319) 362-7483
Fax: (319) 362-7457
www.ruffalocody.com

Provides telephone fundraising, membership, planned giving, consulting and enrollment management services, and software for nonprofit organizations. Among the company's products is CAMPUSCALL software for fundraising, membership, and telecounseling.

FUNDRAISING/TRADE ORGANIZATIONS

American Association of Fundraising Counsel
(see Giving Institute: Leading Consultants to Nonprofits)

American Management Association

1601 Broadway
New York, NY 10019
Phone: (212) 586-8100
Fax: (212) 903-8168
www.amanet.org

Trade group for management professionals, produces free monthly e-newsletters focusing on issues important to managers. Offers an online library, resource center, and more.

Association of Healthcare Philanthropy

313 Park Avenue, Suite 400
Falls Church, VA 22046
Phone: (703) 532-6243
Fax: (703) 532-7170
www.ahp.org

Professional group that offers education and networking for those involved in charitable work related to U.S. healthcare systems.

Association of Fundraising Professionals

1101 King Street, Suite 700
Alexandria, VA 22314
Phone: (703) 684-0410
Fax: (703) 684-0540
www.nsfre.org

The organization provides guidance for professionals responsible for generating support for a nonprofit charitable organization. It developed the "Donor Bill of Rights," detailing what donors should expect from charities, maintains a fundraising resource center, and publishes the annual

"State of Fundraising Survey" as well as "Advancing Philanthropy," a bimonthly magazine.

Association of Philanthropic Counsel (APC)

212 Tryon Street, Suite 1150
Charlotte, NC 28281
Phone: (800) 957-5666
Fax: (704) 365-3678
www.apcinc.org

Promotes best practices and upholds ethical standards in delivery of philanthropic services to nonprofit organizations. Offers professional development and interaction.

Business Committee for the Arts Inc.

29-27 Queens Plaza North, 4th Floor
Long Island City, NY 11101
Phone: (718) 482-9900
Fax: (718) 482-9911
www.bcainc.org

Encourages businesses to support the arts. Offers a variety of publications and a quarterly newsletter.

Council for Advancement and Support of Education (CASE)

1307 New York Avenue NW, Suite 1000
Washington, DC 20005
Phone: (202) 328-2273
Fax: (202) 387-4973
www.case.org

Geared primarily for colleges and private schools, CASE publishes "Currents," which offers ideas for fundraising as well as articles on a variety of academia-related topics. Also publishes books and runs seminars for beginners through seasoned professionals, offers matching gifts products and conference information.

Giving Institute: Leading Consultants to Nonprofits

4700 W. Lake Avenue
Glenview, IL 60025
Phone: (800) 462-2372 or (847) 375-4709
Fax: (866) 609-0913
www.aafrc.org

Professional organization of fundraising consultants. Publishes "Giving USA," an annual summation of national fundraising statistics and trends.

International Association of Fairs and Expositions

3043 East Cairo
Springfield, MO 65802
Phone: (800) 516-0313 or (417) 862-5771
Fax: (417) 862-0156
www.fairsandexpos.com

This nonprofit corporation organizes fairs and expositions. Publishes "Fairs & Expos" magazine, in print and online, which provides details on fairs and expos around the world. A good place to find out if such an event is headed to the charity's area and, if so, attempt to tie a fundraiser to it.

Meeting Professionals International

3030 Lyndon B. Johnson Freeway
Suite 1700
Dallas, TX 75234
Phone: (972) 702-3000
Fax: (972) 702-3070
www.mpiweb.org

This professional educational society serves as a resource for business and meeting professionals. It has a resource center that provides information on how to organize meetings and conventions, the latest industry news, and career management tools.

National Association of Catering Executives

9881 Broken Land Parkway, Suite 101
Columbia, MD 21046
Phone: (410) 290-5410
Fax: (410) 290-5460
www.nace.net

This trade group for food professionals operates a certification program for catering executives, networking, and career enhancement.

National Catholic Development Conference

86 Front Street
Hempstead, NY 11550
Phone: (888) 879-6232 or (516) 481-6000
Fax: (516) 489-9287
www.ncdcusa.org

The major association of Catholic fundraising organizations publishes many timely reports, and offers regional seminars and specialized services.

National Center for Black Philanthropy, Inc.

1828 L Street, N.W., Suite 300
Washington, DC 20036
Phone: (202) 530-9770
Fax: (202) 530-9771
www.ncfbp.net

Promotes giving and volunteerism among African Americans, to foster participation in all aspects of philanthropy, educate the public about the contributions of black philanthropy, strengthen people and institutions engaged in black philanthropy, and research the benefits of black philanthropy to all Americans.

National Society of Fundraising Executives (see Association of Fundraising Professionals)

National Speakers Association

1500 S. Priest Drive
Tempe, AZ 85281
Phone: (480) 968-2552
Fax: (480) 968-0911
www.nsaspeaker.org

Educates professional speakers and helps speakers develop content expertise and professionalism.

Professional Convention Management Association

2301 S. Lake Shore Drive, Suite 1001
Chicago, IL 60616
Phone: (877) 827-7262 or (312) 423-7262
Fax: (312) 423-7222
www.pcma.org

A nonprofit organization that promotes education and networking for meeting professionals.

Public Relations Society of America

33 Maiden Lane, 11th Floor
New York, NY 10038
Phone: (212) 460-1400
Fax: (212) 995-0757
www.prsa.org

The largest organization for public relations professionals offers professional development resources including a magazine for senior management and public relations executives, newsletters, seminars, and conferences.

Toastmasters International

23182 Arroyo Vista
Rancho Santa Margarita, CA 92688
Phone: (949) 858-8255
Fax: (949) 858-1207
www.toastmasters.org

Trains speakers for nonprofit education leadership and communications. Offers various publications.

ONLINE RESOURCES

Donor Town Square

P.O. Box 156
Crozet, VA 22932
Phone: (434) 509-4240
Fax: (866) 744-6588
www.donortownsquare.com

Provides economical and easy-to-use online donation pages. Accounts can be set up in minutes without a monthly or setup fee. A small monthly fee is charged for an advanced fundraising account and customized donation page html.

eInvite.com

216 W. Boylston Street
West Boylston, MA 01583
Phone: (888) 346-8463
www.einvite.com

Offers holiday greeting cards program for fundraisers.

Givezilla

www.givezilla.com

A for-profit company that partners with Amazon.com to enable nonprofit organizations to retain as much as 10 percent of product sales made on their Web sites.

PROMOTIONAL MATERIALS

Blue Sky Marketing

633 Skokie Blvd, Suite 100LL
Northbrook, IL 60062
Phone: (847) 562-0777
Fax: (847) 562-0111
www.buybluesky.com

Blue Sky Marketing offers promotional products for sales incentives, and awards items starting at 25 cents to name brands offering custom design projects.

CharityCDs.com /CustomDiscs.com

1 Stavebank Road N, 2nd Floor
Mississauga, ON L5G 2T3 Canada
Phone: (866) 826-1100, ext. 333
Fax: (647) 271-0073
www.customdiscs.com

Provides music CDs featuring customized liner booklets to promote the organization's message alongside top artists' songs. Themed titles are available for smaller orders (1,200 units), with custom-tailored repertoire for larger runs.

PUBLICATIONS

Chronicle of Philanthropy

1255 23rd Street, Suite 700
Washington, DC 20037
Phone: (202) 466-1200
Fax: (202) 466-1200
www.philanthropy.com

This biweekly newspaper offers news and information on fundraisers and other aspects of the nonprofit world. It offers lots of resource materials, including "The Nonprofit Handbook," grant listings, and other tools.

Fundraising Success Magazine

1500 Spring Garden Street, Suite 1200
Philadelphia, PA 19130
Phone: (973) 956-8585
Fax: (973) 956-7757
www.fundraisingsuccessmag.com

Provides nonprofits with practical information, strategies, and expert advice.

Fundraisinginfo.com

3520 Piedmont Road N.E., Suite 300
Atlanta, GA 30305
Phone: (877) 637-5889
Fax: (404) 524-2992
www.fundraisinginfo.com

Offers how-to guides, samples, expert advice, in-depth prospect profiles, fundraising news, and related materials.

International Events Group (IEG)

640 N. LaSalle, Suite 450
Chicago, IL 60610
Phone: (312) 944-1727
Fax: (312) 458-7111
www.sponsorship.com

Compiles substantial resources invaluable to fundraisers. Publishes an annual guide to the 4,500 most active sponsors, what they like to sponsor, sponsorship opportunities, and hundreds of event marketing agencies and industry suppliers. Gives seminars online and in person.

New York Publicity Outlets Directory

Bacon's Information
332 S. Michigan Avenue, Chicago, IL 60604
Phone: (866) 639-5087
www.bacons.com

This doyenne of directories has been around for close to 50 years. The semi-annual directory details who does what in New York City's broadcast and print organizations. There are listings for thousands of media outlets and key media contacts at newspapers, magazines, broadcast and cable TV networks, radio, news services, and ethnic and community publications.

Metro California Media

Bacon's Information
332 S. Michigan Avenue
Chicago, IL 60604
Phone: (866) 639-5087

Special Events Magazine

17383 Sunset Boulevard, Suite A220
Pacific Palisades, CA 90272
Phone: (800) 543-4116 or (310) 230-7160
Fax: (31) 230-7168
www.specialevents.com

Publishes a monthly magazine, annual product and source guide, and weekly e-newsletter. Materials include menu inspiration, practical tips, sales-building strategies, and business management tips.

The NonProfit Times

201 Littleton Road, 2nd Floor
Morris Plains, NJ 07950
Phone: (973) 401-0202
Fax: (973) 401-0404
www.nptimes.com

Publishes "The NonProfit Times," "Exempt" magazine, NPTimes.com, and the "NPT Weekly," "NPT Instant Fundraising," and "NPT Jobs" e-mail newsletters all geared to nonprofit executives, covering all aspects of the nonprofit organization focusing on news, management, fundraising, and finances.

Philanthropy Journal

220 Fayetteville St. Mall, Suite 300, P.O. Box 12800
Raleigh, NC 27605
Phone: (800) 853-0801
Fax: (919) 890-6279
www.philanthropyjournal.org

Aims to help people understand, support, and work in the nonprofit and philanthropic world. Through a daily Web site and free, weekly e-mail bulletin, delivers news, information, and opinions about charitable giving and fundraising.

Variety

360 Park Avenue South
New York, NY 10010
Phone: (866) MYVARIETY
www.variety.com

The trade magazine for the entertainment field.

Wiley & Sons Inc.

111 River Street
Hoboken, NJ 07030
Phone: (201) 748-6000
Fax: (201) 748-6088
www.wiley.com

Wiley and Jossey-Bass (an imprint of Wiley) are the publishers of the Nonprofit Management Series, which is designed to meet the information needs of nonprofit professionals. Wiley and Jossey-Bass authors offer ideas, insights, and tools in nonprofit leadership and management to help fundraisers tackle the issues they confront every day.

SOFTWARE

Access International

432 Columbia Street, Suite B05
Cambridge, MA 02141
Phone: (617) 494-0066
Fax: (617) 494-8404
www.accessint.com

The Enterprise Fundraising & CRM System supports all aspects of a development office including membership, annual fund, capital campaigns; direct marketing, major gift cultivation, planned gift management, special events, ticketing, and much more.

Agilon

3801 Beverly Road, SW
Cedar Rapids, IA 52409
Phone: (800) 480-9015
www.myagilon.com

Provides Web-based software for fundraising and relationship management, offering comprehensive solutions for fundraising, fund accounting, prospect and campaign management, memberships, on-line communities, e-mail communication solutions, and events management.

Blackbaud

2000 Daniel Island Drive
Charleston, SC 29492
Phone: (800) 443-9441
Fax: (843) 216-6100
www.blackbaud.com

Blackbaud is a leading provider of software and related services designed specifically for nonprofit organizations. Best known for its flagship fundraising solution, The Raiser's Edge, Blackbaud also offers solutions and consulting services for financial management, Web site management, prospect research, business intelligence, school administration, and ticketing.

Contribute.com

805 S.W. Broadway, Suite 1600
Portland, OR 97205
Phone: (503) 973-5200
Fax: (503) 973-5252
www.contribute.com

Offers affordable, easy-to-use fundraising management software, which complements the company's online processing service. The company custom builds online forms so donors can make contributions, register for events, or become a member from a charity's Web site.

Convio, Inc.

11921 N. Mopac Expressway, Suite 200
Austin, TX 78759
Phone: (888) 528-9501, ext. 1
Fax: (512) 652-2699
www.convio.com

Provides Internet software and services for nonprofits, with solutions for fundraising and membership, advocacy, special events, volunteer fundraising, Web site management, and e-mail communications. Products include an online marketing database that centralizes constituent data and synchronizes with offline databases, delivering a unified view of constituent interests.

DonorPerfect Fundraising Software, Inc.

540 Pennsylvania Ave., #200
Fort Washington, PA 19034
Phone: (800) 220-8111
Fax: (215) 628-0585
www.donorperfect.com

The company offers Web- and PC-based fundraising software to manage annual appeals, capital campaigns, and special events. Among the features is WebLink, which allows secure online forms for donations, inquiries, sign-ups, and more.

Easy-Ware Corporation

2052 N Lincoln Park West #614
Chicago, IL 60614
Phone: (773) 755-7732
Fax: (773) 442-0410
www.easy-ware.com

Easy-Ware sells Total Info, a constituent management program for nonprofit organizations that handles fundraising, membership, volunteers, events/auctions, contact management, e-mail, calendar, grant management, schools, camp, box office, letters, reports, mailing labels, and more.

eTapestry Inc.

5455 Harrison Park Lane
Indianapolis, IN 46216
Phone: (317) 545-4170
Fax: (317) 545-4180
www.etapestry.com

Offers Web-based fundraising and donor management software that can be accessed from any Internet connection and all updates, maintenance, and data backups are automatically provided. Additional products and services include advanced e-mail, online giving, WishList, and Web site development and hosting.

MatchMaker FundRaising Software

5225 N. Central Avenue, Suite 208
Phoenix, AZ 85012
Phone: (800) 752-3100
Fax: (602) 265-6688
www.matchmakerfrs.com

Offers a fully integrated software application designed for fundraising professionals by fundraising professionals. The program features gift, pledge, and event management, plus volunteer and grant tracking. MatchMaker has an extensive tickler note system, unlimited capacity for donor attributes, and generates more than 130 reports.

TowerCare Technologies

8500 Brooktree Road, Suite 230
Wexford, PA 15090
Phone: (724) 935-8281
Fax: (724) 935-8283
www.towercare.com

DonorPro combines functions such as donor management, volunteer management, and auction management, into one easy-to-learn and use package.

TRAVEL SOURCES

Academic Travel Abroad, Inc.

1920 N Street, N.W., Suite 200
Washington, DC 20036
Phone: (800) 556-7896
Fax: (202) 342-0317
Web: academic-travel.com

Academic Travel Abroad, Inc. (ATA) is an international tour operator that assists development professionals in using travel as a fundraising tool. It specializes in custom-designed travel programs to destinations abroad for sophisticated cultural and nonprofit organizations.

Mitch-Stuart, Inc.—Destinations of Excellence

28202 Cabot Road, Suite 225
Laguna Niguel, CA 92677
Phone: (800) 574-9991
Fax: (949) 276-9997
www.mitchstuart.com

Provides a variety of auction travel packages that charities need not purchase in advance.

YTB Travel & Cruises Inc.

12716 S. Constance Street
Olathe, KA 66062
Phone: (866) 742-9824
www.ytbassociations.com

The company offers a travel affinity program for fundraising for nonprofit organizations. The company develops private label Web sites for organizations, enabling supporters and members to book both business and leisure travel online.

WEB-SITE MANAGEMENT

BrowserMedia

7735 Old Georgetown Road, Suite 500
Bethesda, MD 20814
Phone: (301) 656-1144, ext. 175
Fax: (301) 656-2772
www.browsermedia.com

Manages and designs Web content for nonprofit and member-based organizations, including strategy, design, development, hosting, and maintenance.

Donor Town Square, Inc

P.O. Box 156
Crozet, VA 22932
Phone: (434) 509-4240
Fax: (866) 744-6588
www.donortownsquare.com

Donor Town Square provides online donation pages that are flexible, secure, reliable, and affordable. Online accounts can be set up quickly without a monthly or set-up fee. For a small monthly fee, set up an advanced fundraising account and customized donation page html. Provides Web-site hosting and design services.

Index